TOP COUNTRY

Page	Song	Artist
2	American Soldier	TOBY KEITH
6	Beer for My Horses	TOBY KEITH with WILLIE NELSON
10	Help Pour Out the Rain (Lacey's Song)	BUDDY JEWELL
18	In a Real Love	PHIL VASSAR
22	Long Black Train	JOSH TURNER
15	Me and You	KENNY CHESNEY
26	Mud on the Tires	BRAD PAISLEY
52	Party for Two	SHANIA TWAIN with BILLY CURRINGTON
30	Redneck Woman	GRETCHEN WILSON
34	Remember When	ALAN JACKSON
38	This One's for the Girls	MARTINA McBRIDE
42	Travelin' Soldier	DIXIE CHICKS
48	Walking in Memphis	LONESTAR

ISBN 0-634-09548-X

7777 W. BLUEMOUND RD. P.O. BOX 13819 MILWAUKEE, WI 53213

For all works contained herein:
Unauthorized copying, arranging, adapting, recording or public performance is an infringement of copyright.
Infringers are liable under the law.

Visit Hal Leonard Online at
www.halleonard.com

American Soldier

Words and Music by Toby Keith and Chuck Cannon

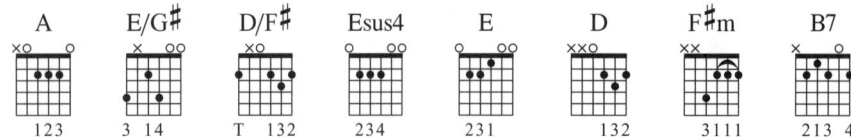

Strum Pattern: 1
Pick Pattern: 1

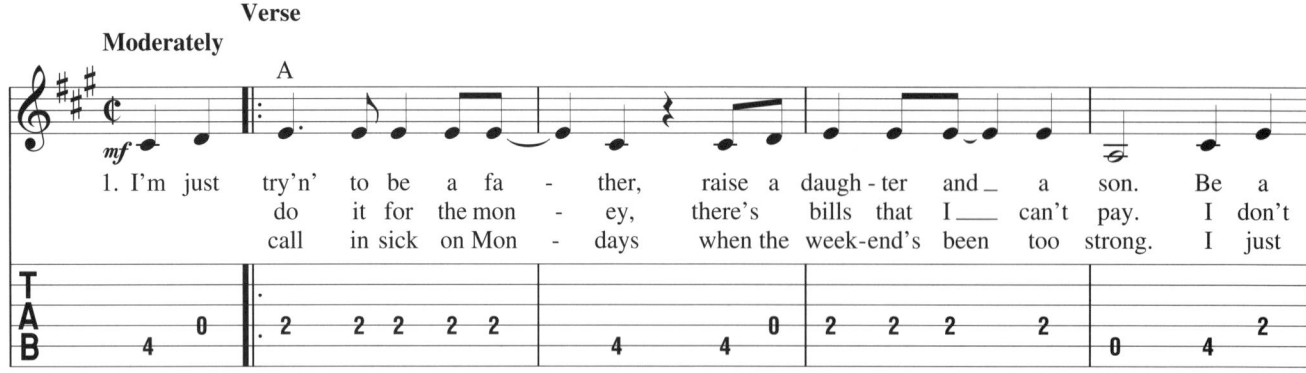

1. I'm just try'n' to be a father, raise a daughter and a son. Be a lover to their mother. Ev'rything to ev'ryone. Up and at 'em bright and early, I'm all bus'ness in my suit. Yeah, I'm dressed up for success from my head down to my boots.

2. I don't do it for the money, there's bills that I can't pay. I don't do it for the glory, I just do it anyway. Providing for our future's my responsibility. Yeah, I'm real good under pressure bein' all that I can be.

3. And I can't call in sick on Mondays when the weekend's been too strong. I just work straight through the holidays, sometimes all night long. You can bet that I stand ready when the wolf growls at the door. Hey, I'm solid, hey, I'm steady, hey, I'm

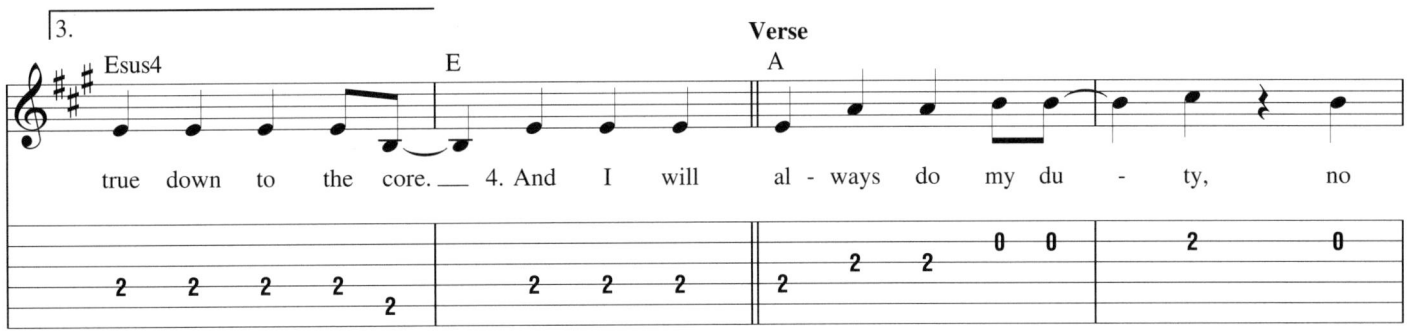
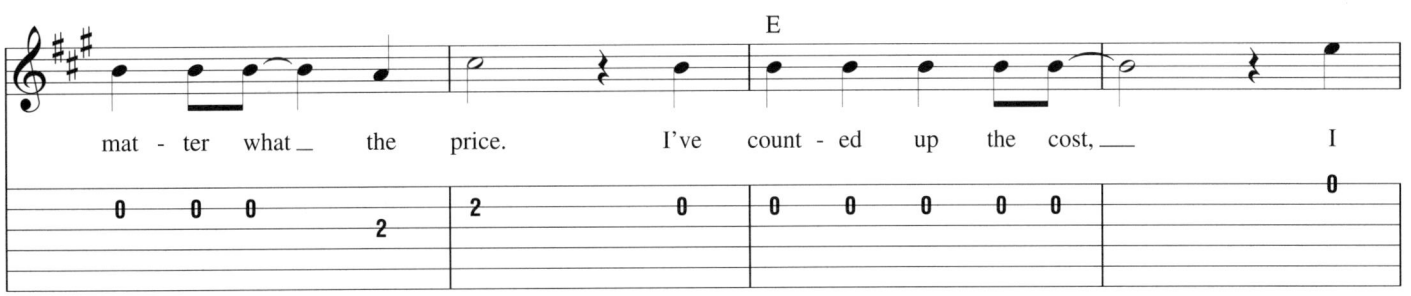
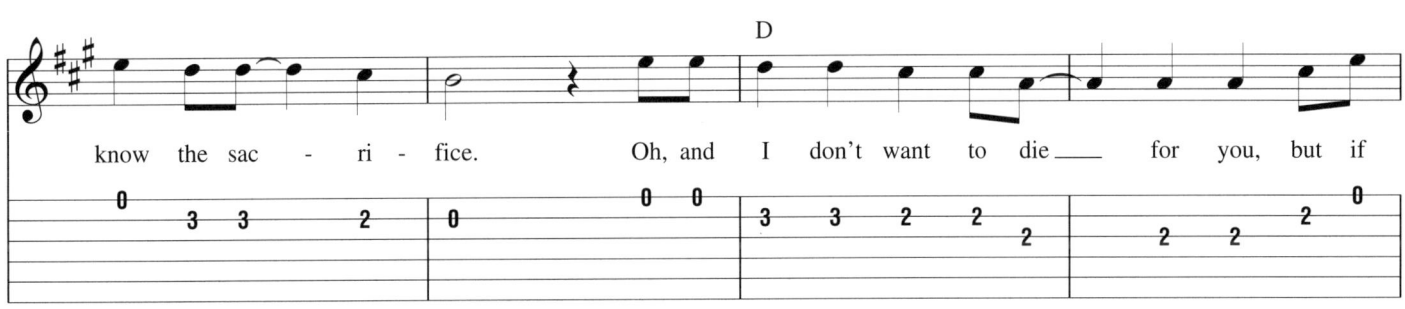

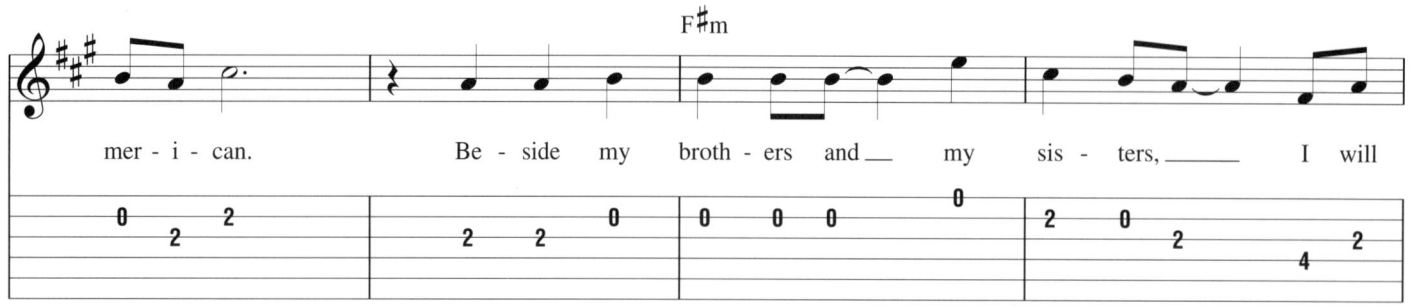
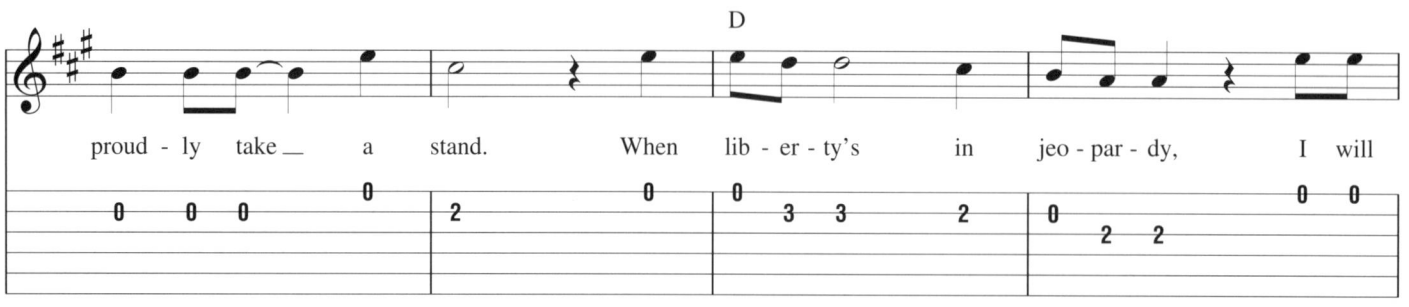
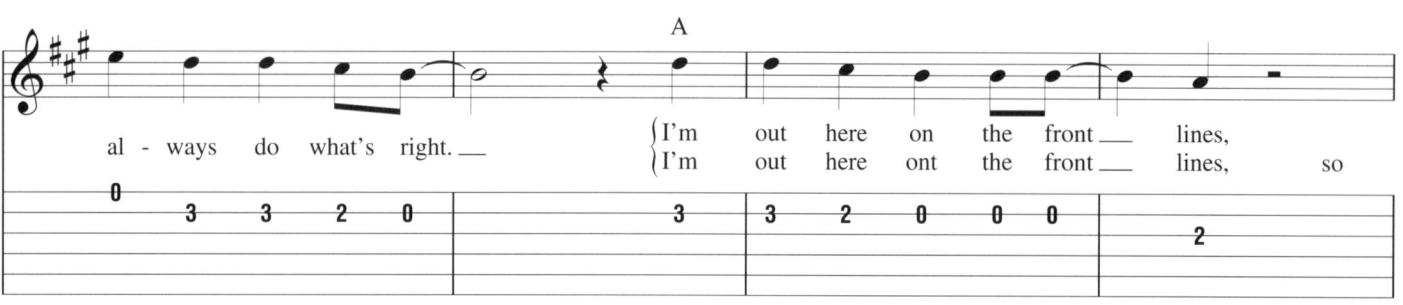
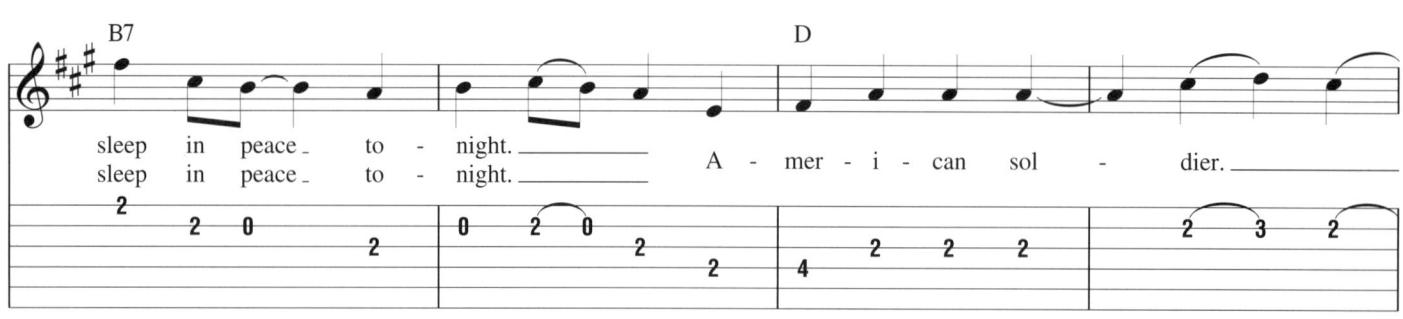
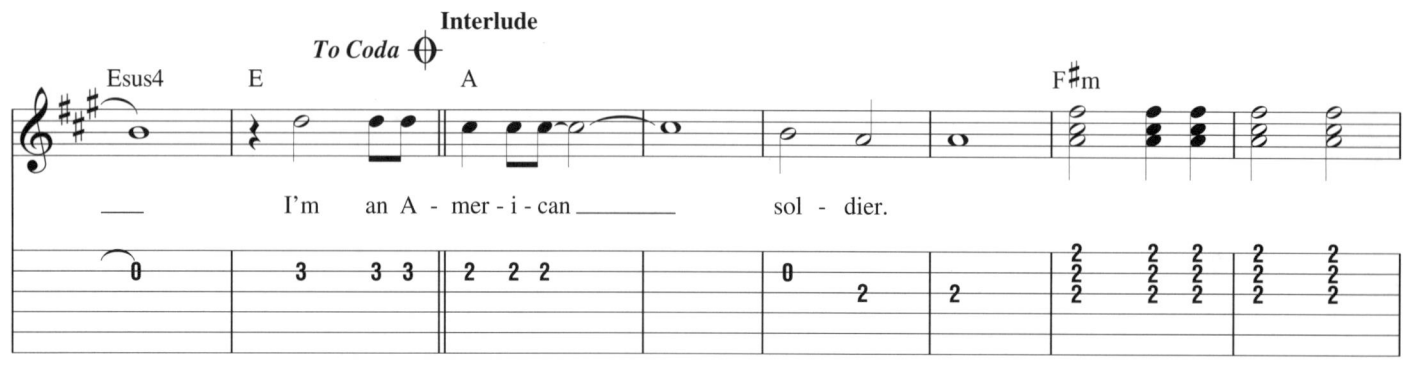

Beer for My Horses

Words and Music by Toby Keith and Scott Emerick

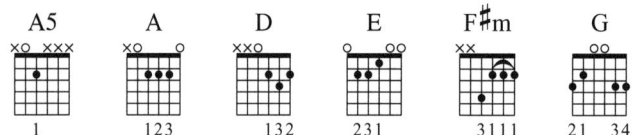

*Capo I

Strum Pattern: 1
Pick Pattern: 3

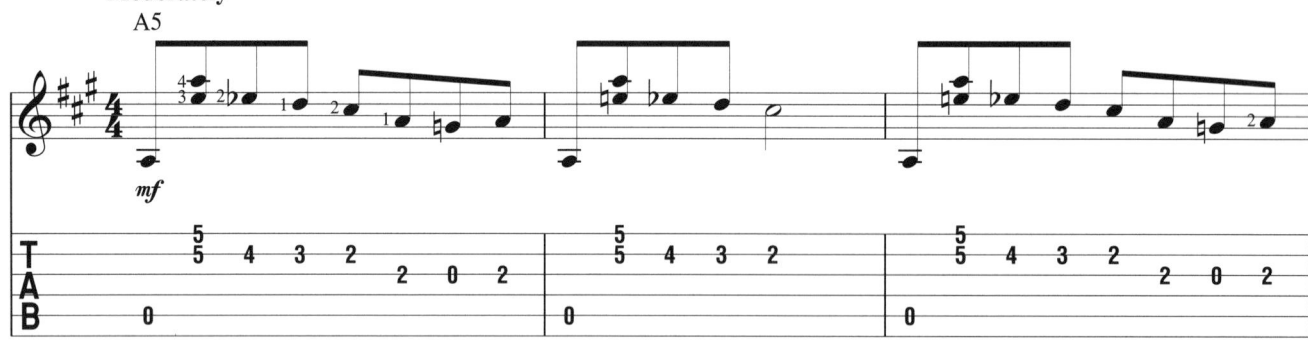

*Optional: To match recording, place capo at 1st fret.

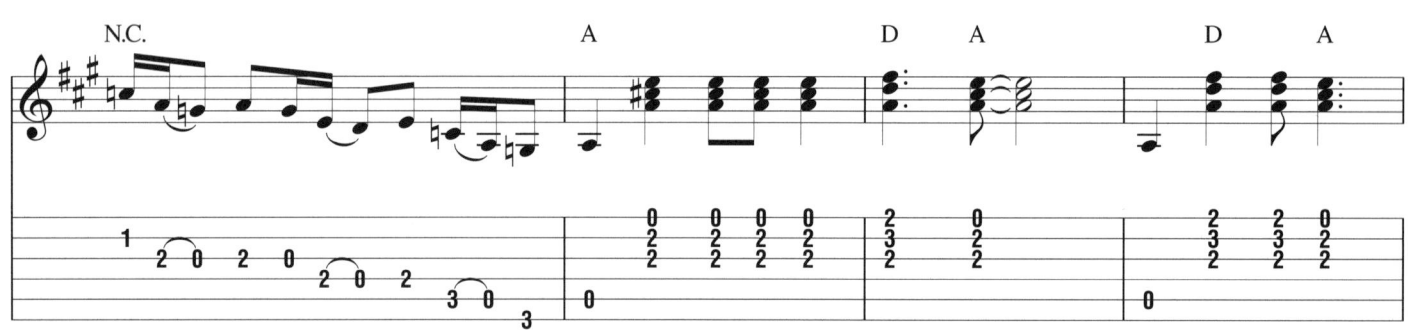

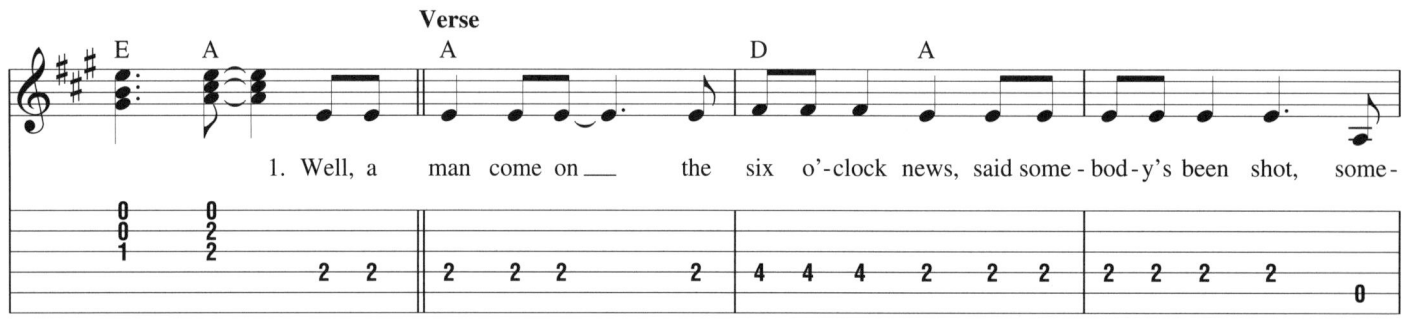

1. Well, a man come on the six o'clock news, said somebody's been shot, some-

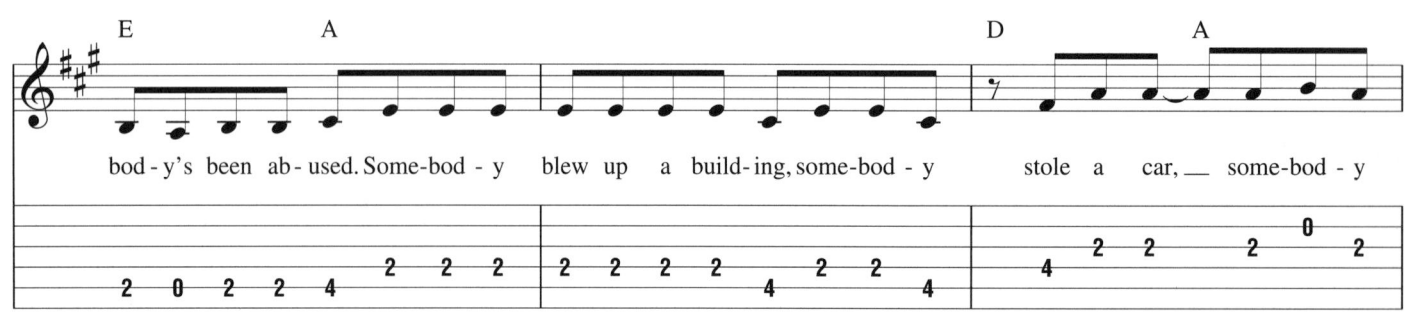

body's been abused. Somebody blew up a building, somebody stole a car, somebody

Copyright © 2002 Tokeco Tunes, Sony/ATV Songs LLC and Big Yellow Dog Music
All Rights on behalf of Sony/ATV Songs LLC and Big Yellow Dog Music Administered by
Sony/ATV Music Publishing, 8 Music Square West, Nashville, TN 37203
All Rights Reserved   Used by Permission

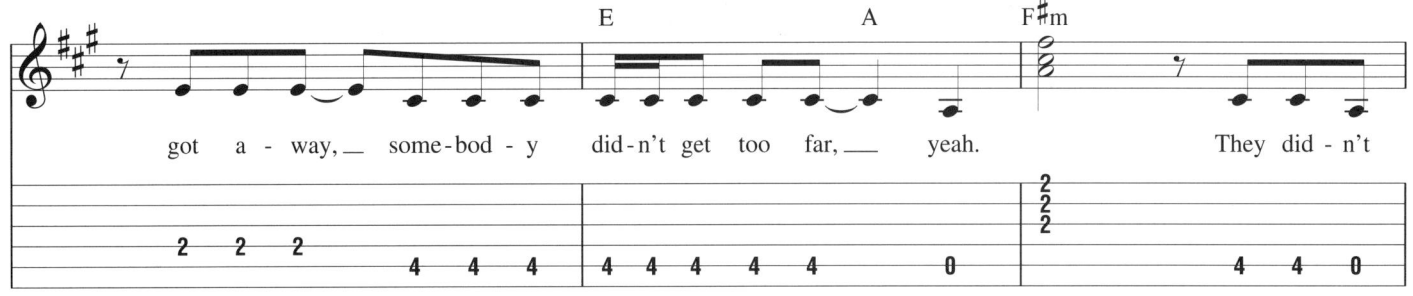

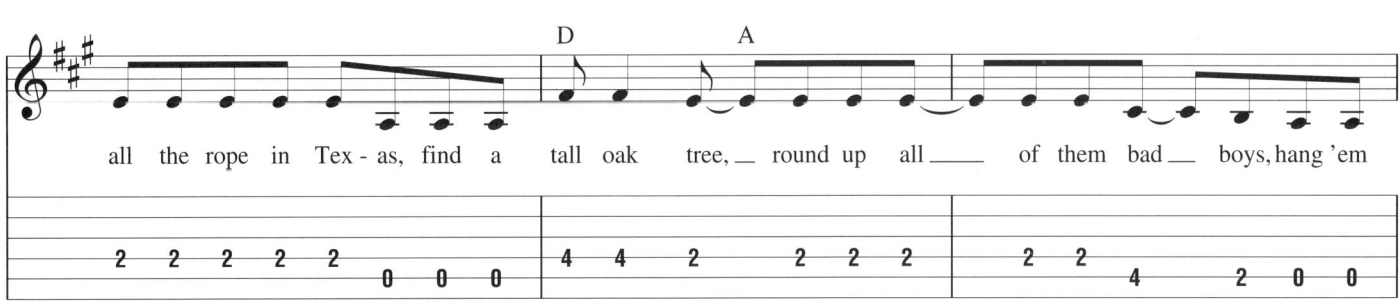
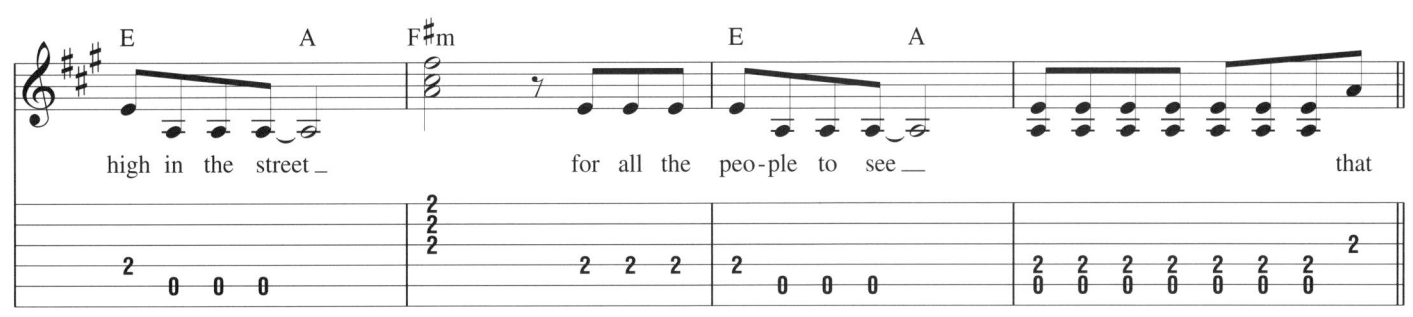

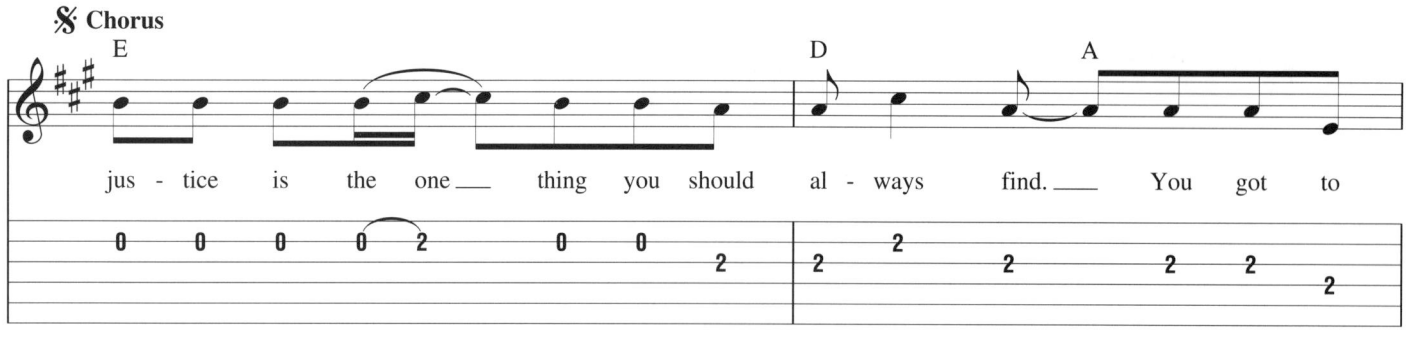
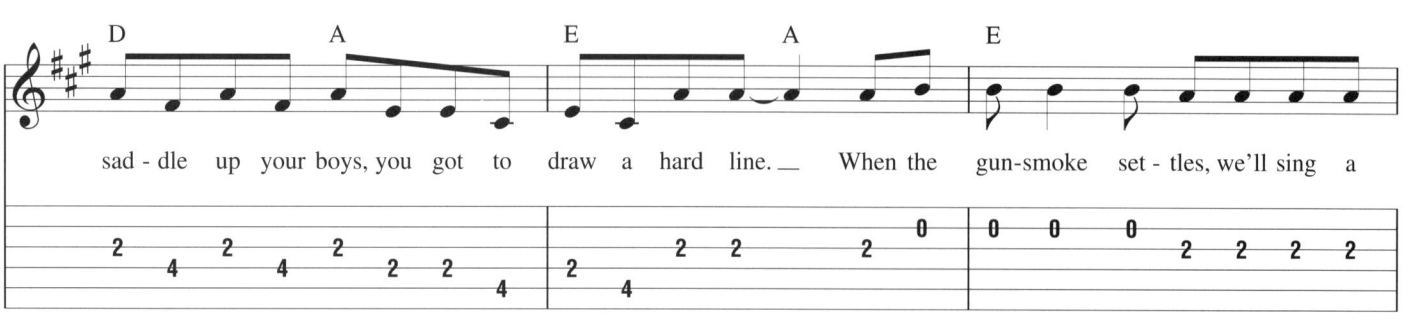
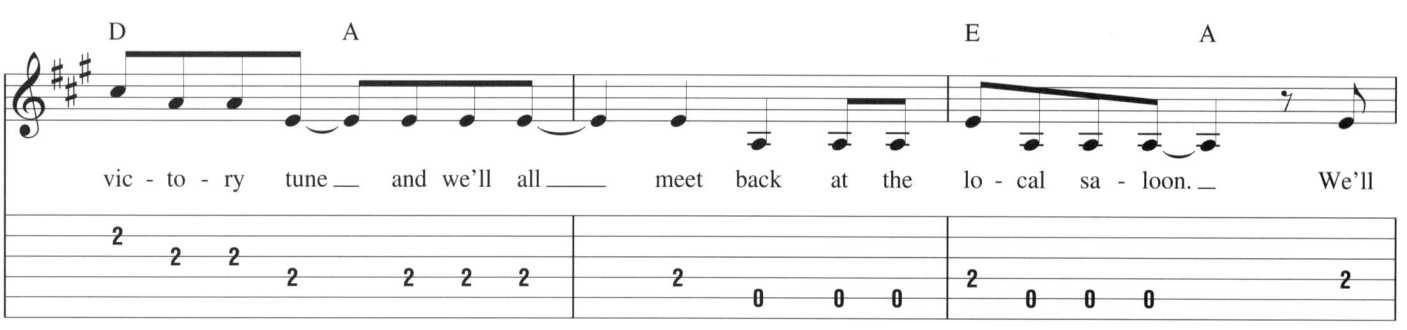
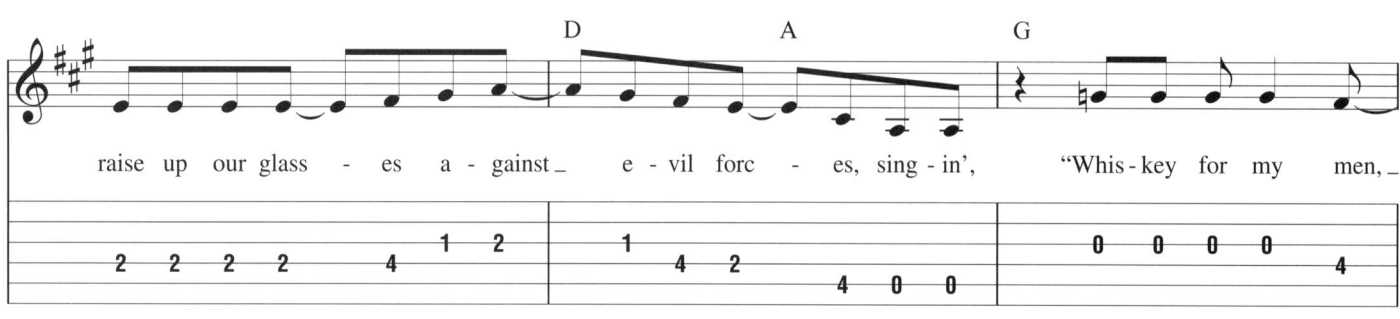
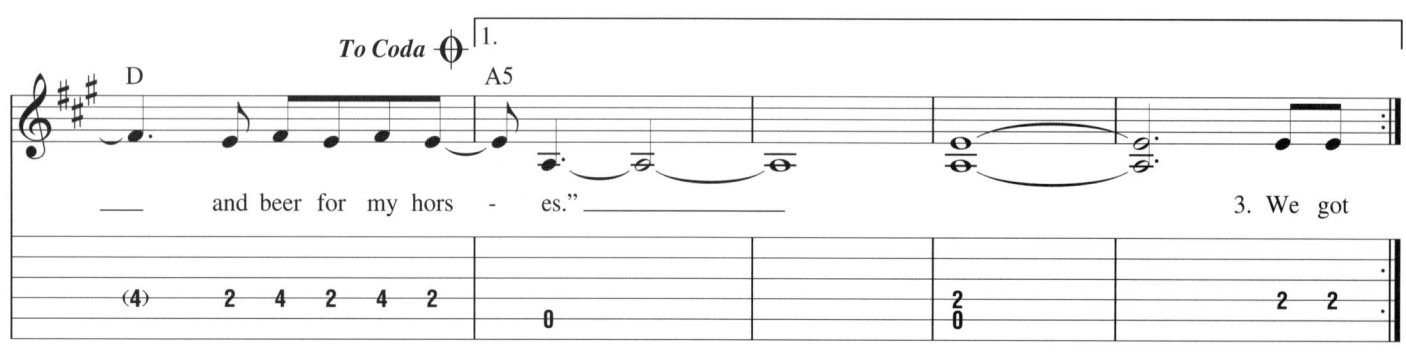

Additional Lyrics

3. We got too many gangsters doing dirty deeds,
   Too much corruption and crime in the streets.
   It's time the long arm of the law put a few more in the ground,
   Send 'em all to their Maker and He'll settle 'em down.
   You can bet He'll set 'em down, 'cause...

Help Pour Out the Rain
(Lacey's Song)

Words and Music by Buddy Jewell

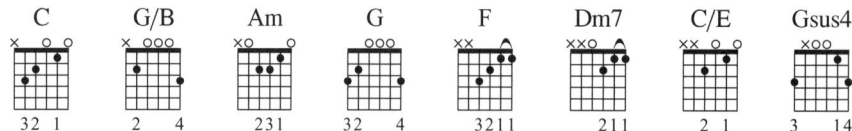

Strum Pattern: 3
Pick Pattern: 1

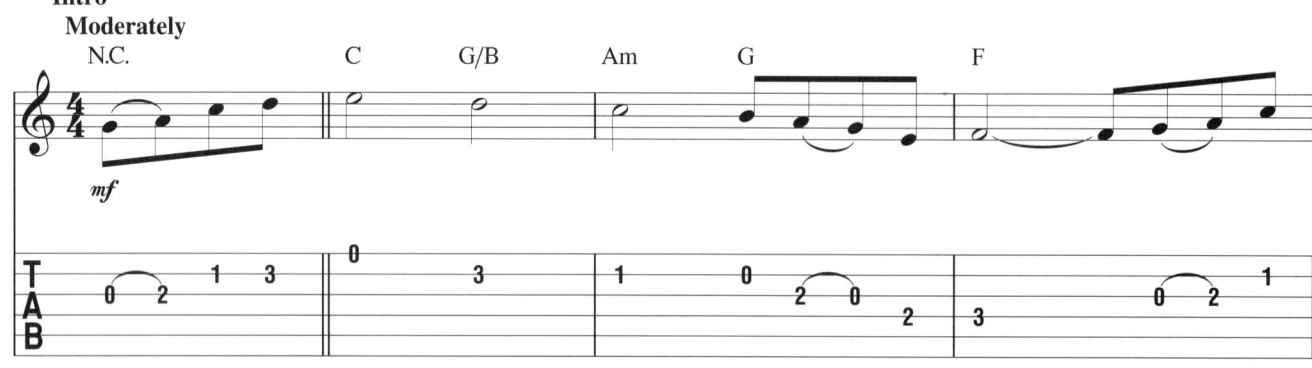

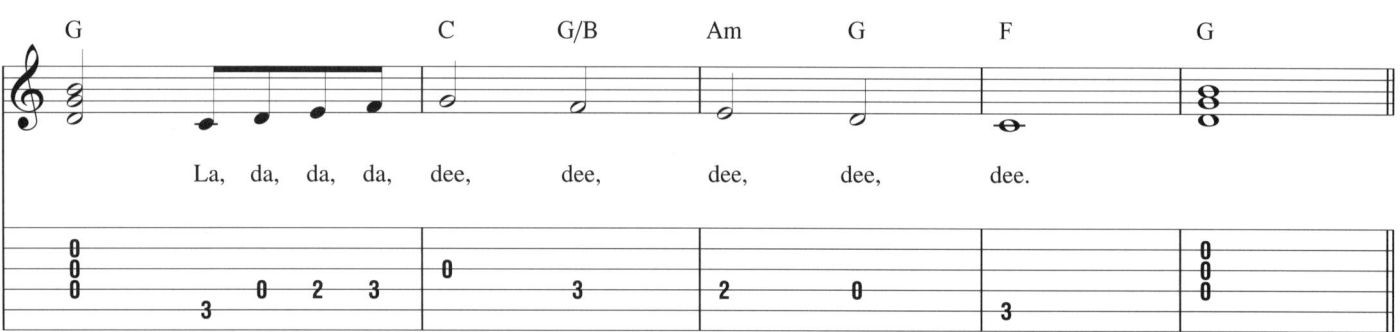

La, da, da, da, dee, dee, dee, dee, dee.

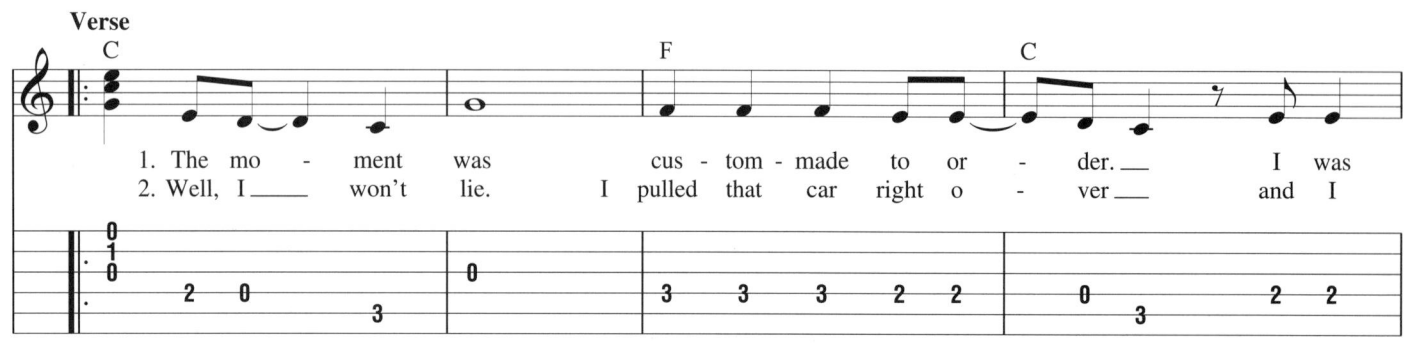

1. The mo-ment was cus-tom-made to or-der. I was
2. Well, I won't lie. I pulled that car right o-ver and I

Copyright © 2003 Sony/ATV Songs LLC, Reveille B Music Publishing and My Little Jewel Music
All Rights Administered by Sony/ATV Music Publishing, 8 Music Square West, Nashville, TN 37203
International Copyright Secured All Rights Reserved

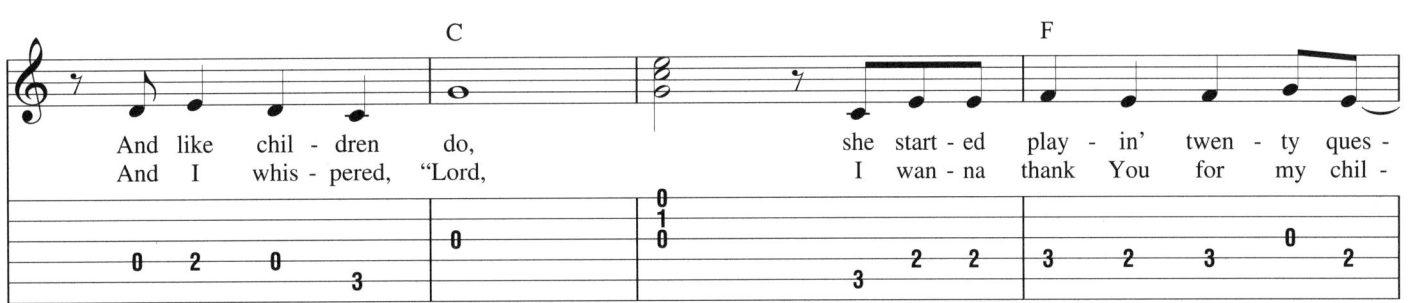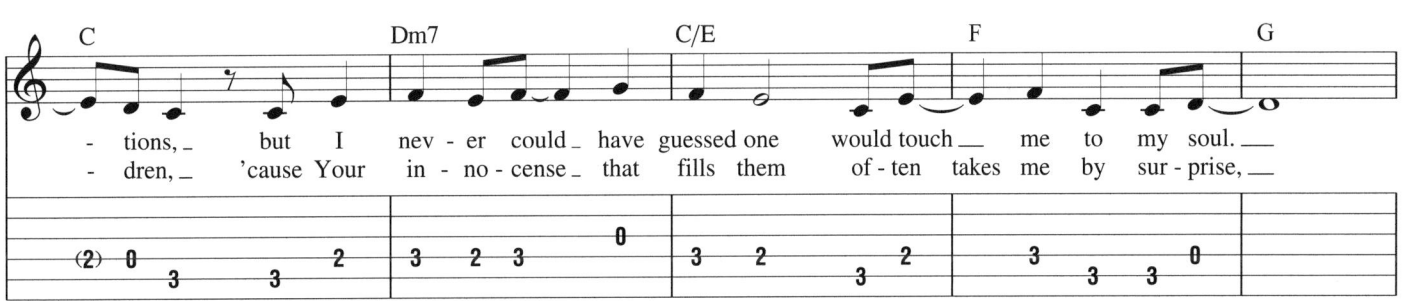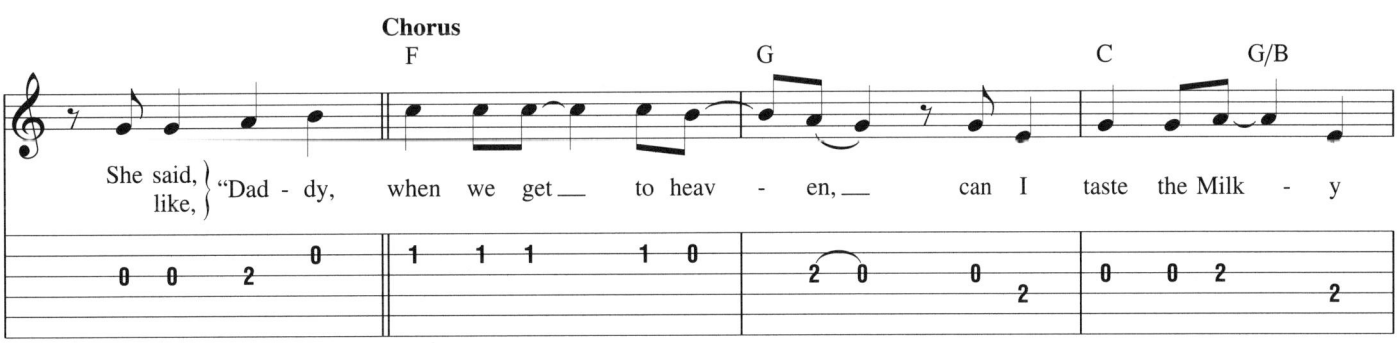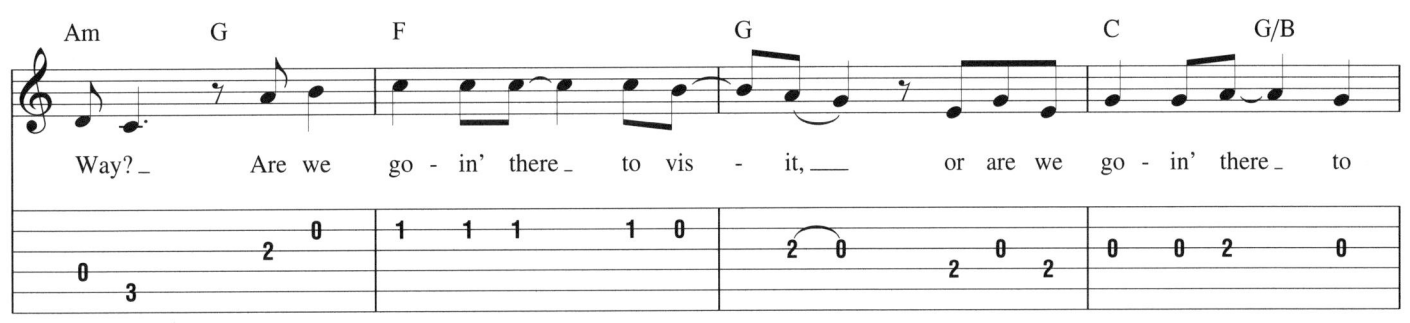

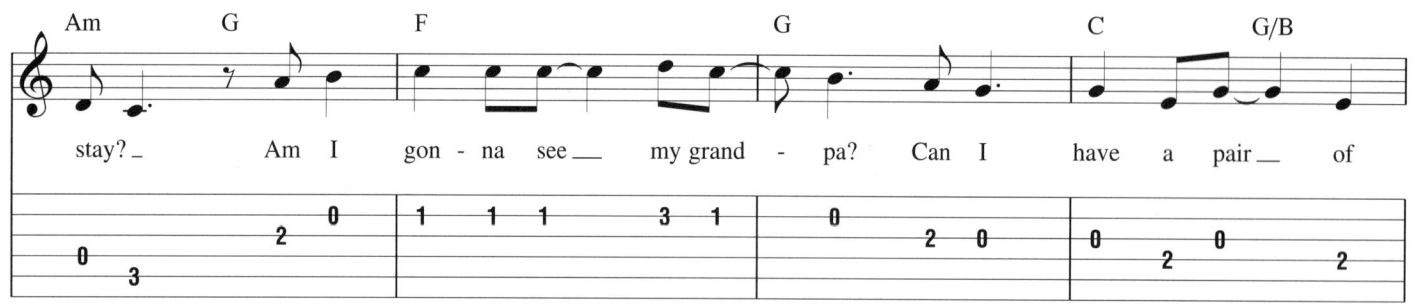

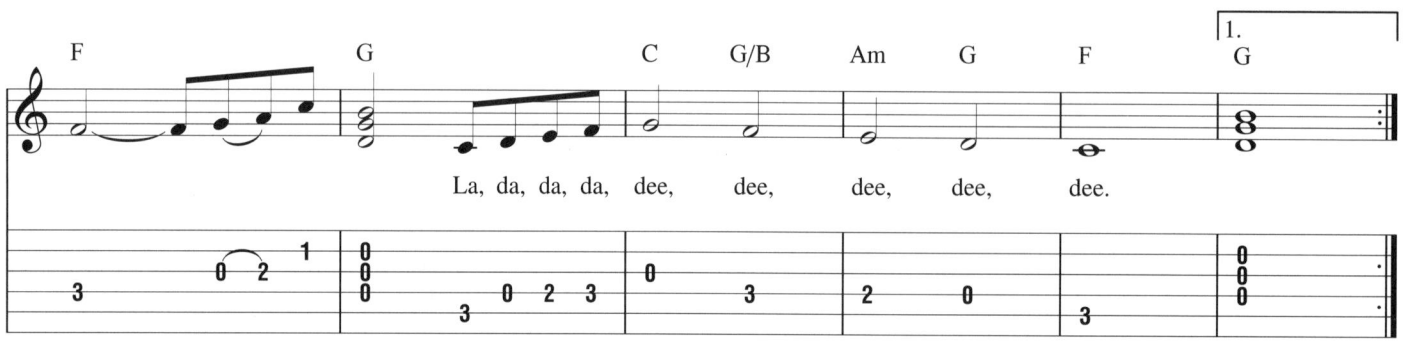
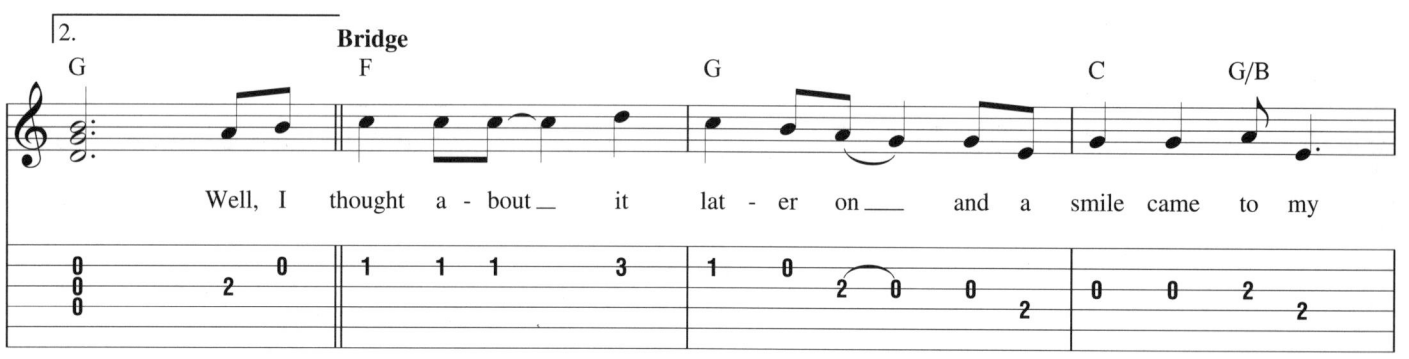

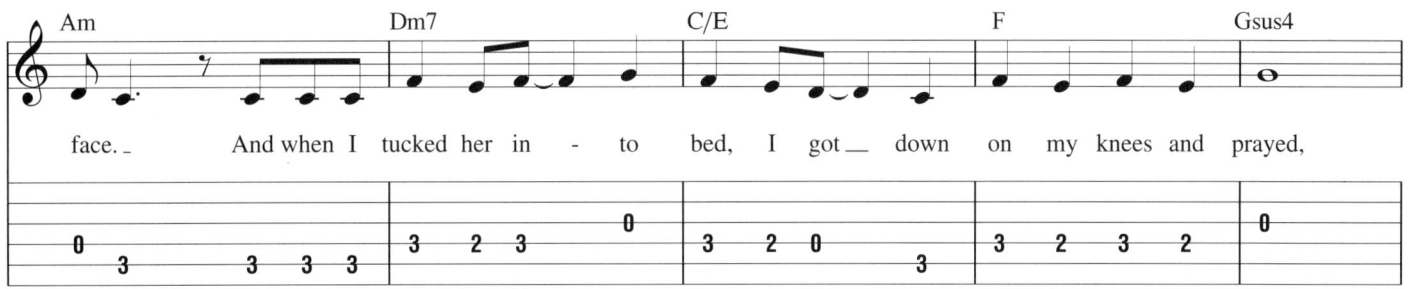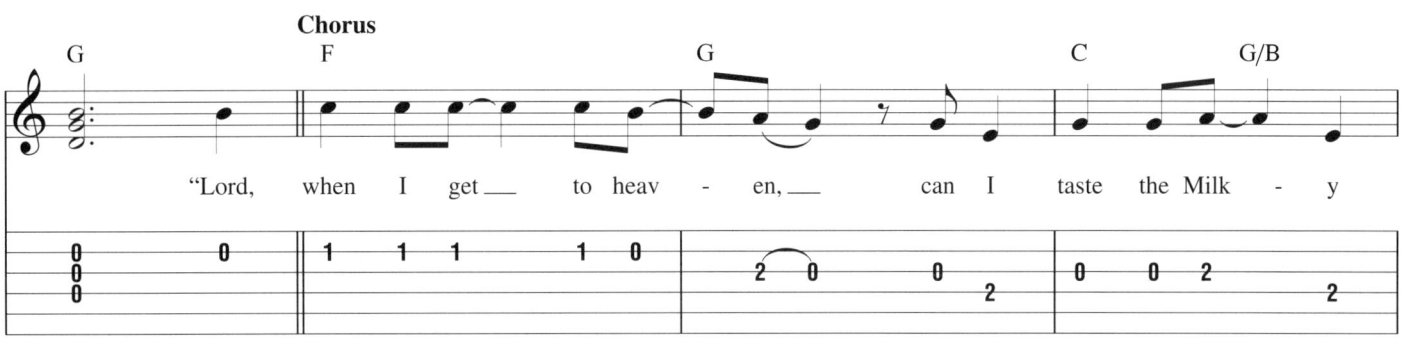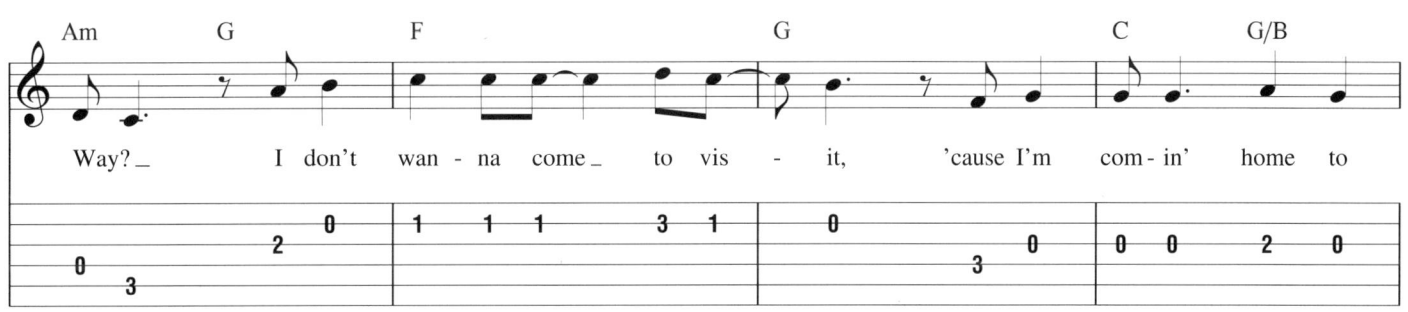

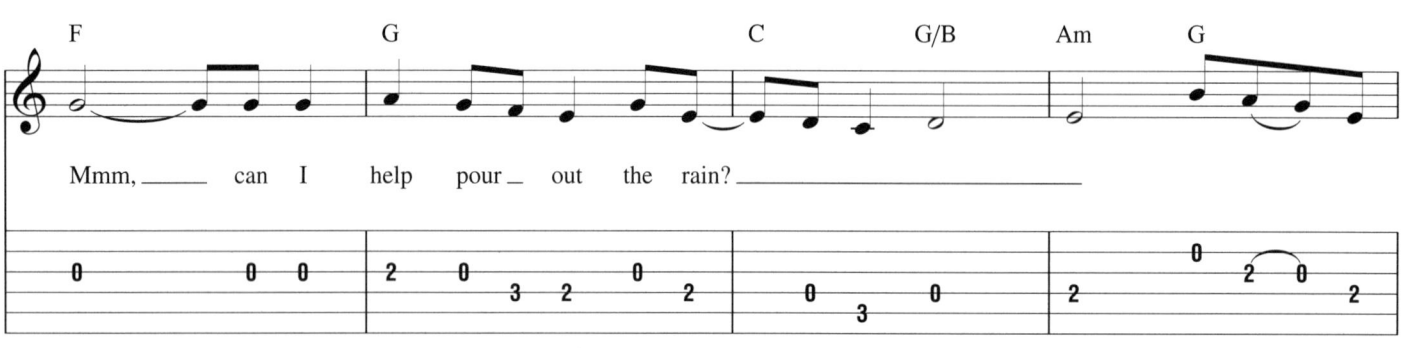
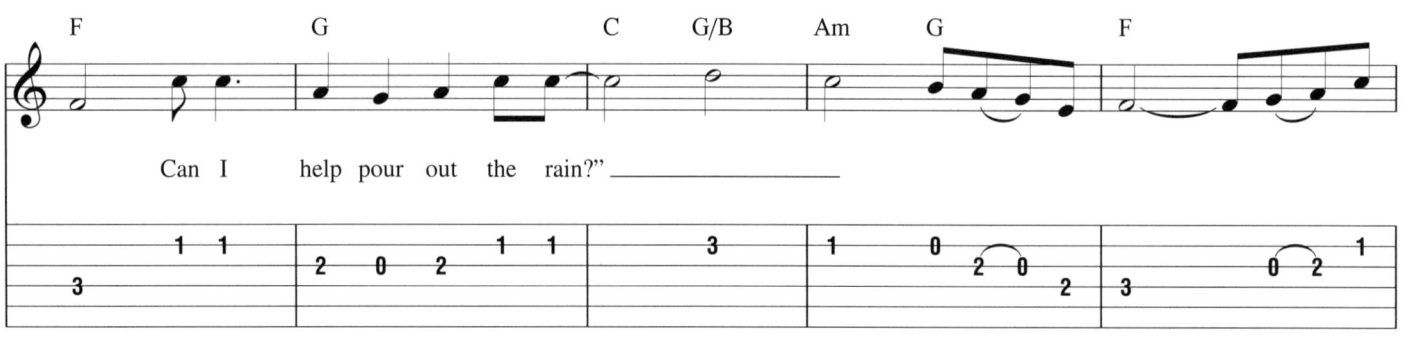
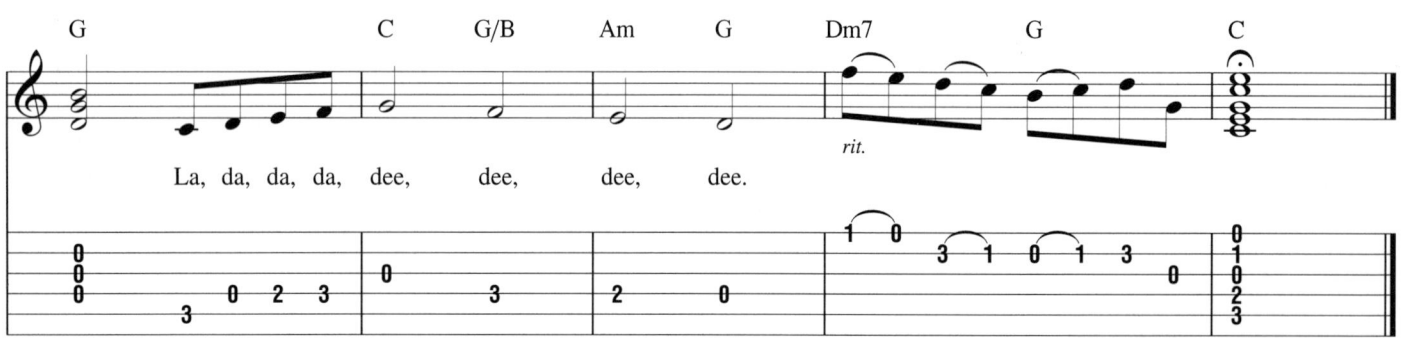

Me and You

Words and Music by Skip Ewing and Ray Herndon

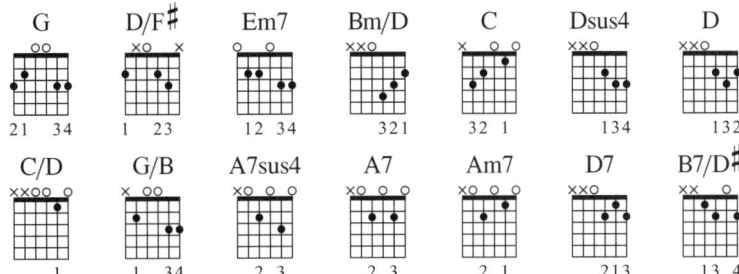

Strum Pattern: 1
Pick Pattern: 3

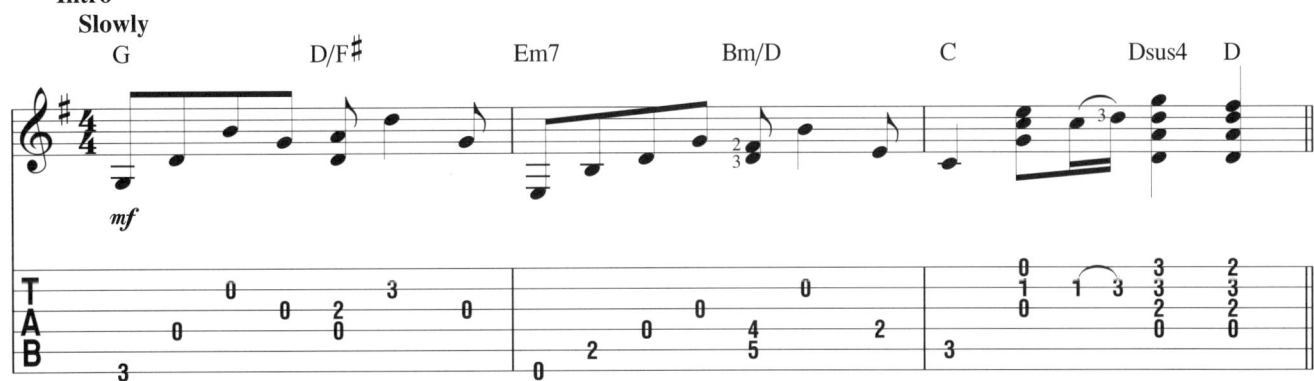

1. Or - di - nar - y? No, real - ly don't think so, not a love this true.
2. Like a per - fect scene from a mov - ie screen, we're a dream come true.

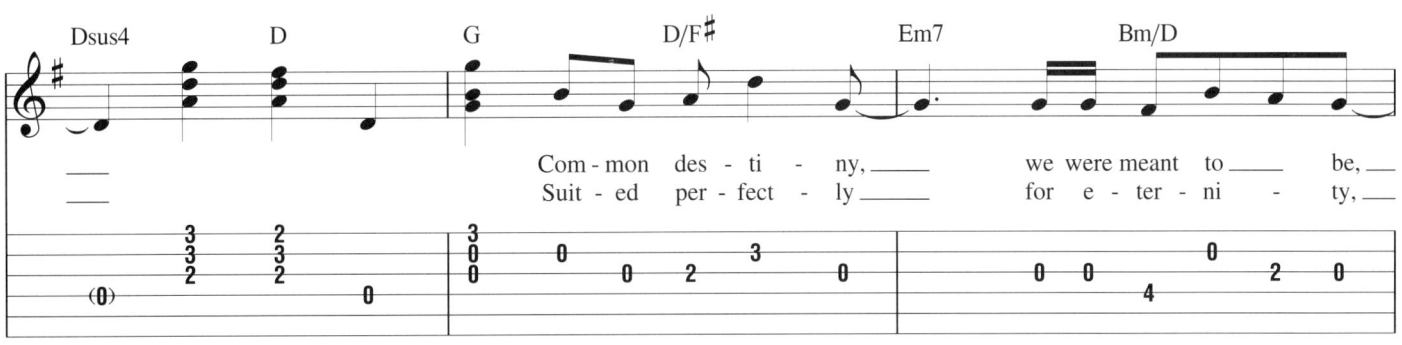

Com - mon des - ti - ny, we were meant to be,
Suit - ed per - fect - ly for e - ter - ni - ty,

Copyright © 1995 Sony/ATV Songs LLC
All Rights Administered by Sony/ATV Music Publishing, 8 Music Square West, Nashville, TN 37203
International Copyright Secured   All Rights Reserved

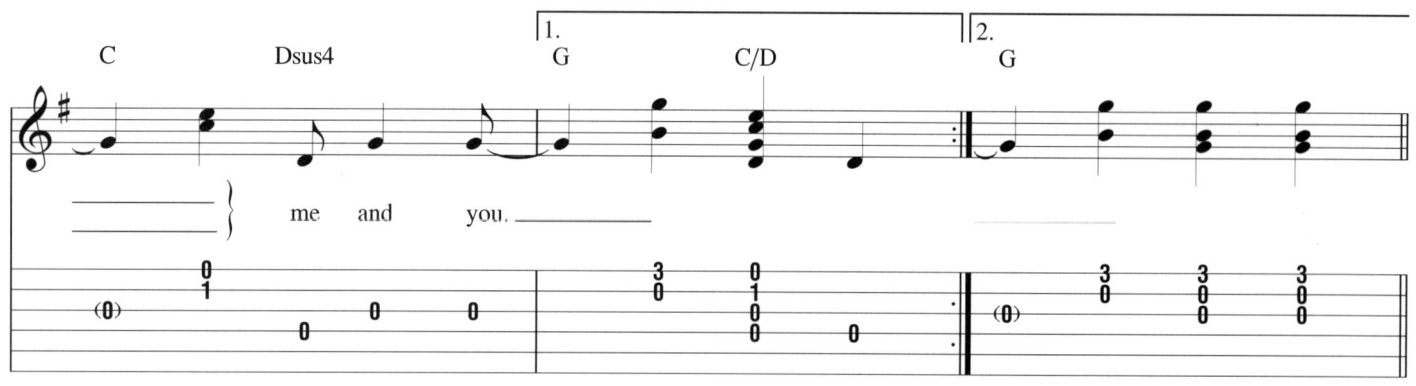

*Use Pattern 10

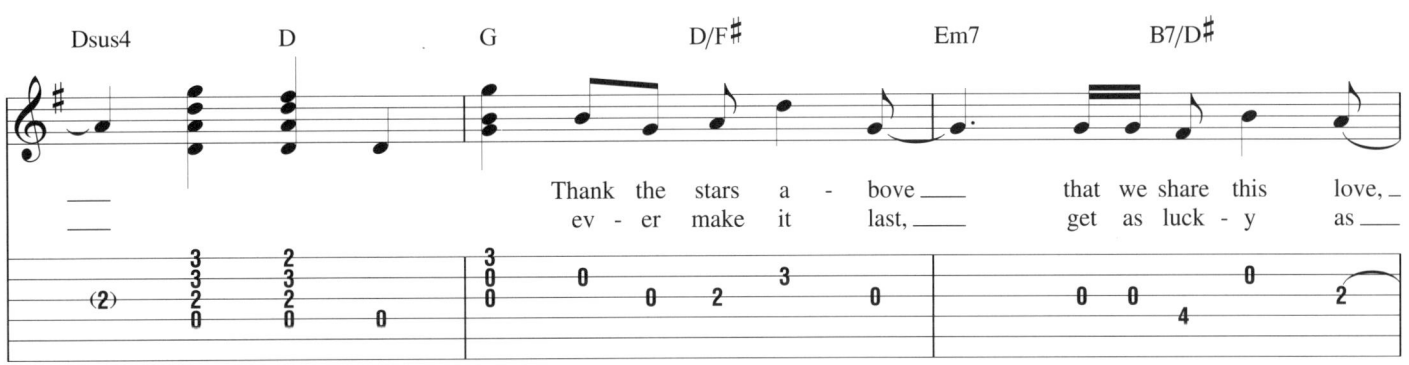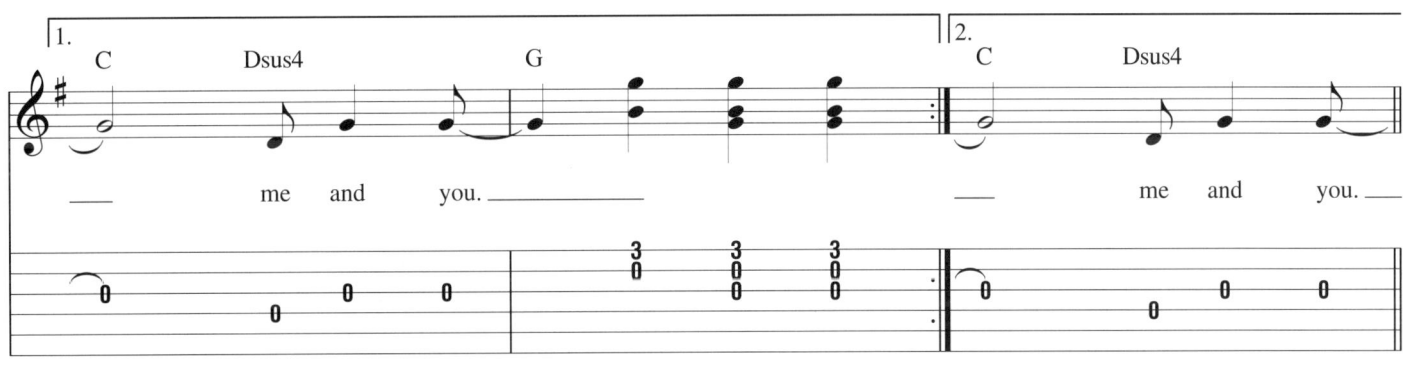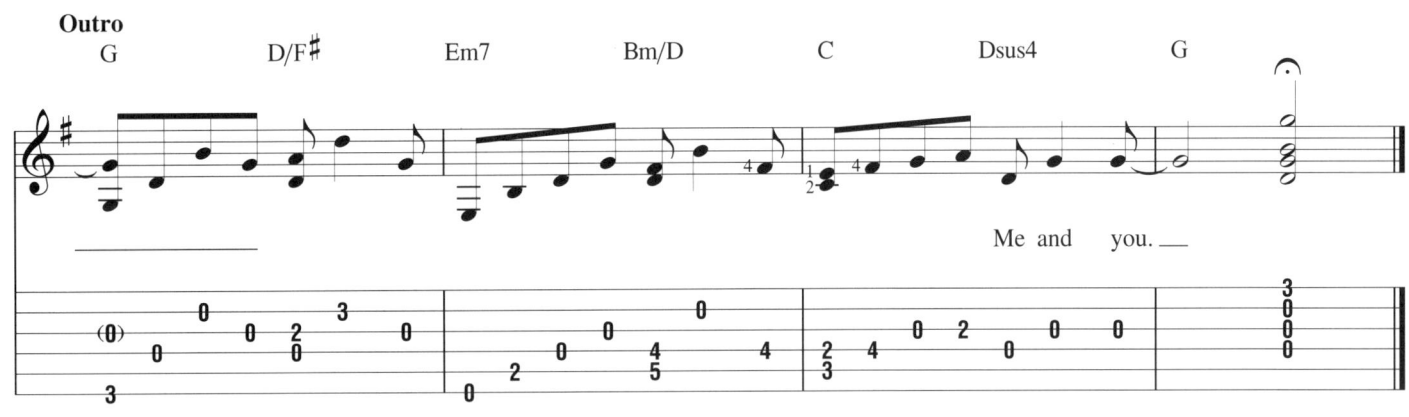

In a Real Love

Words and Music by Phil Vassar and Craig Wiseman

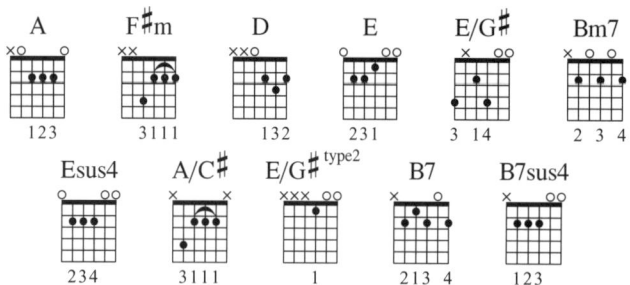

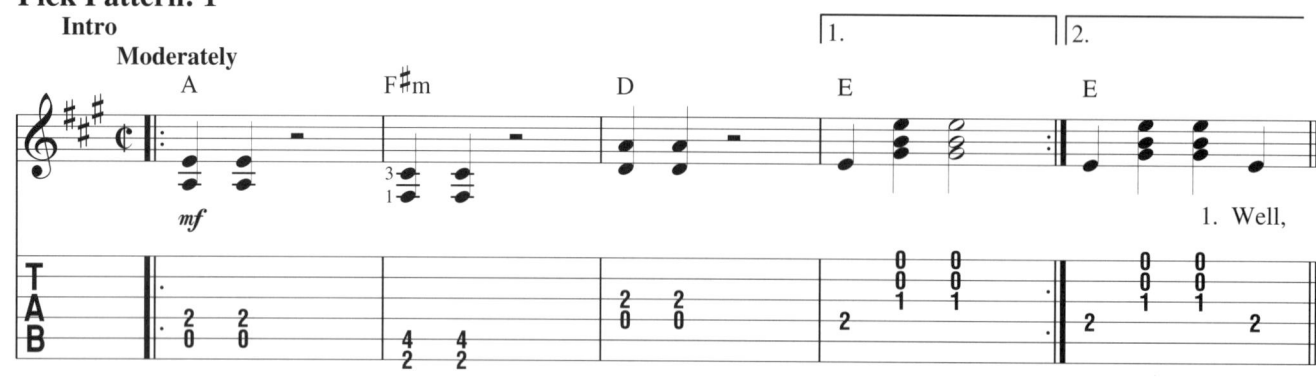

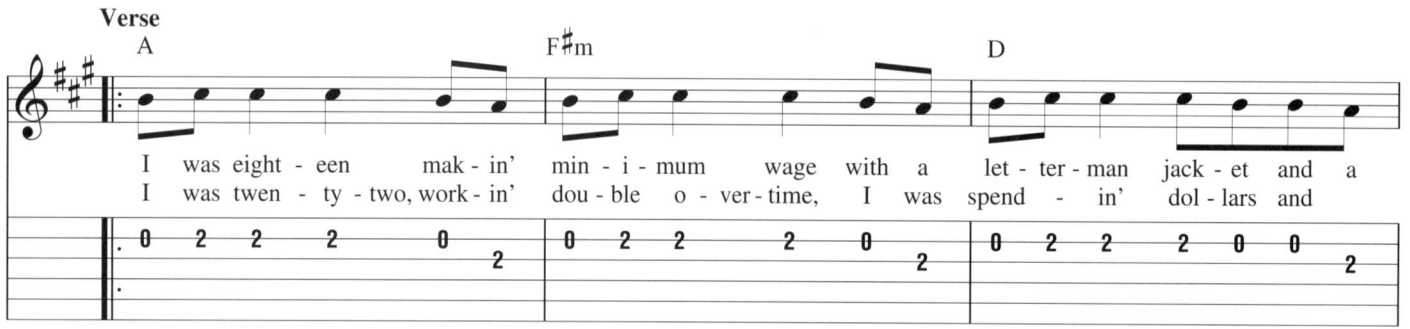

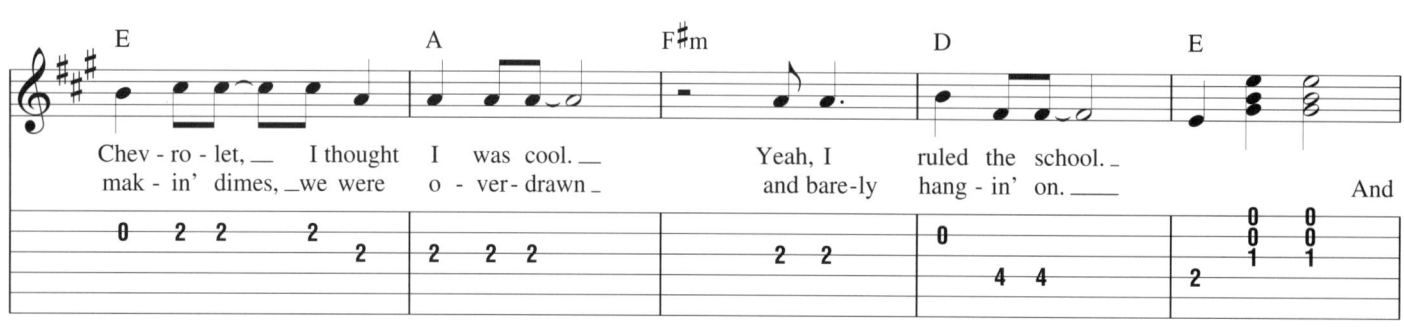

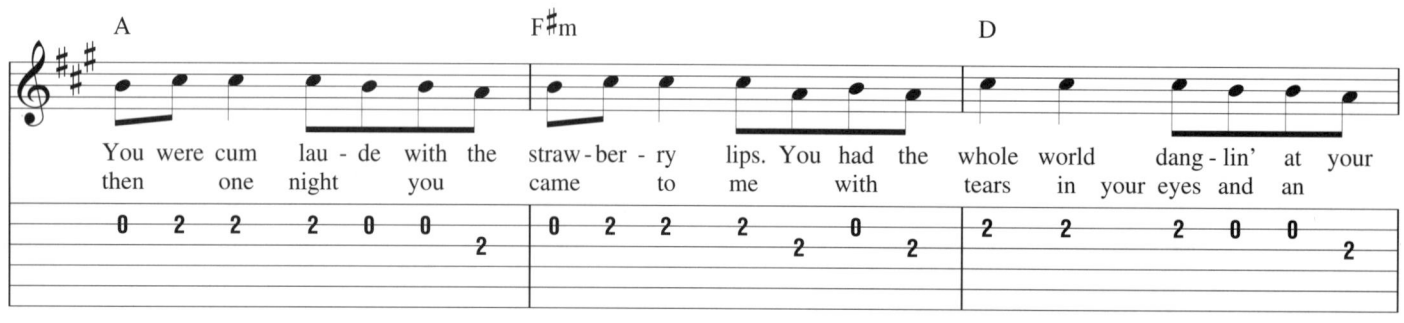

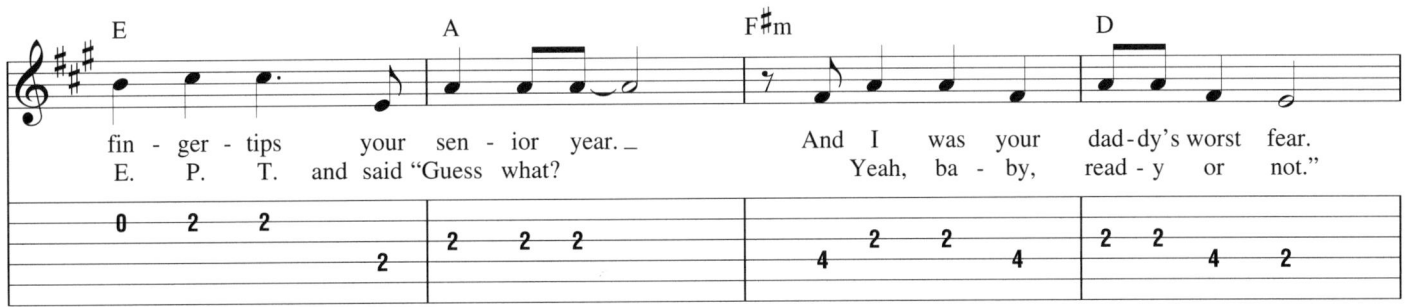
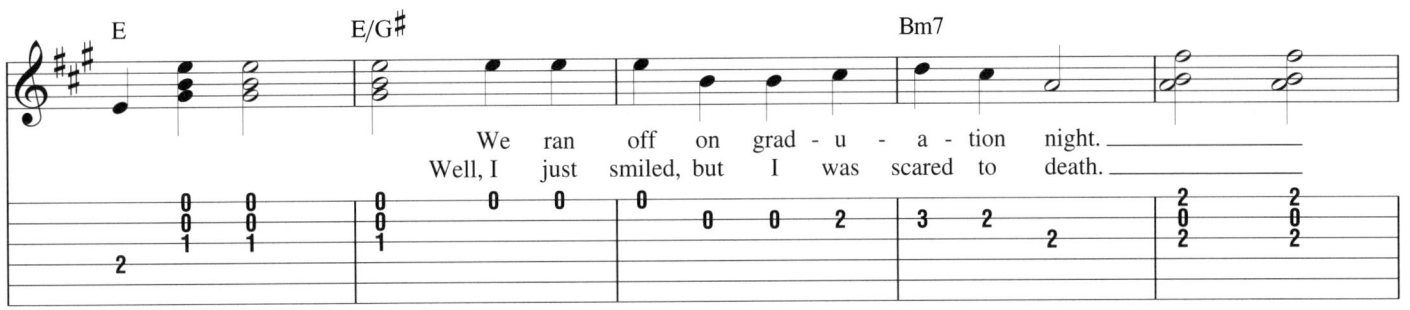

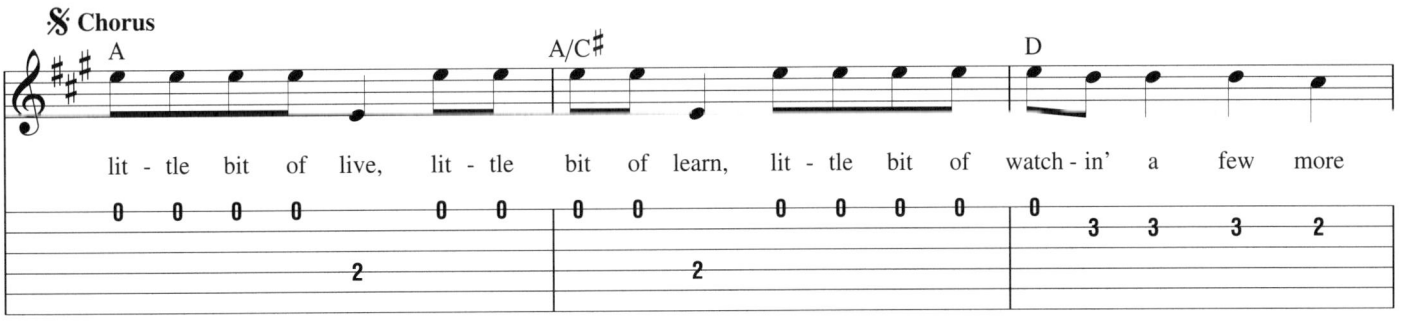
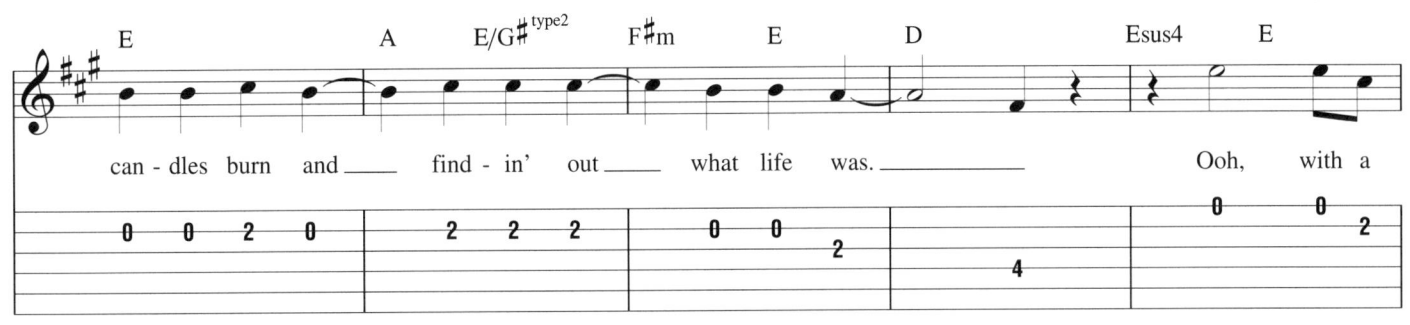

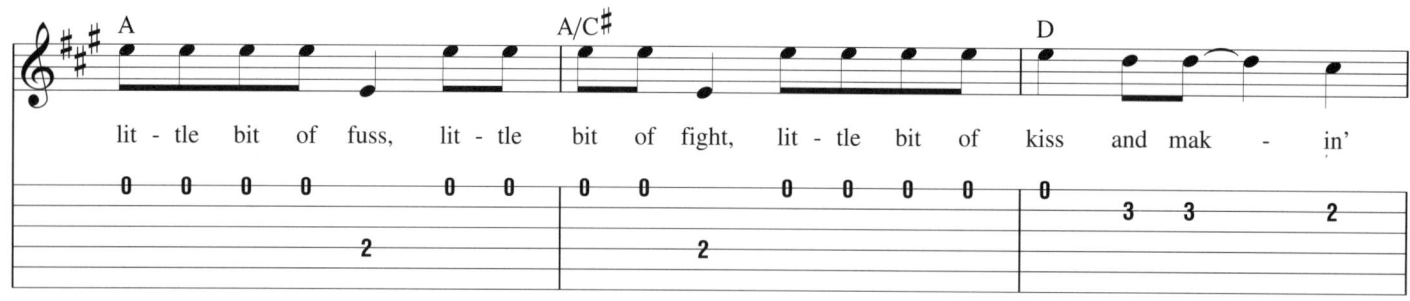
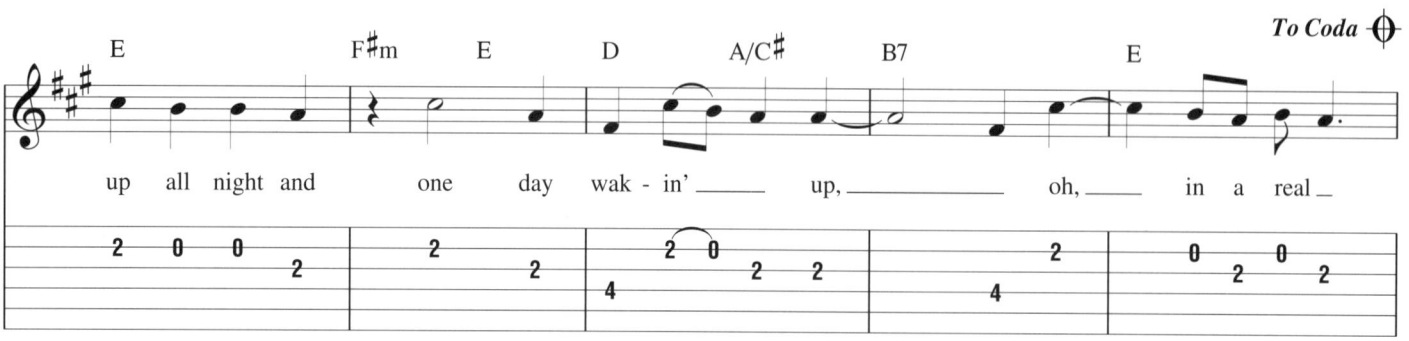
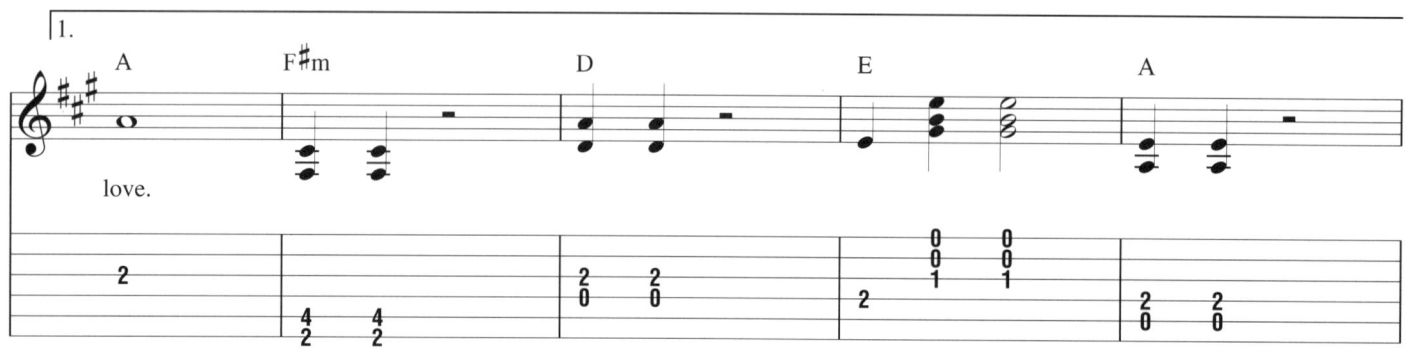
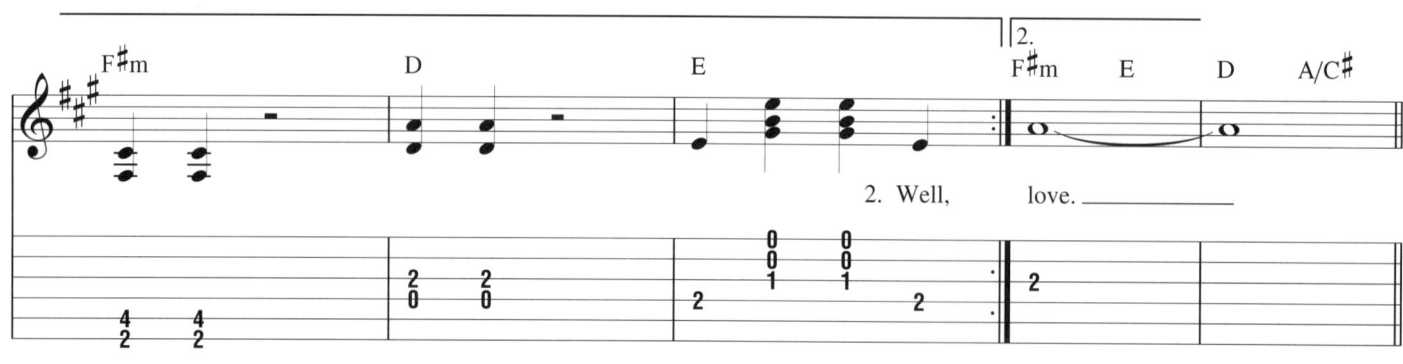

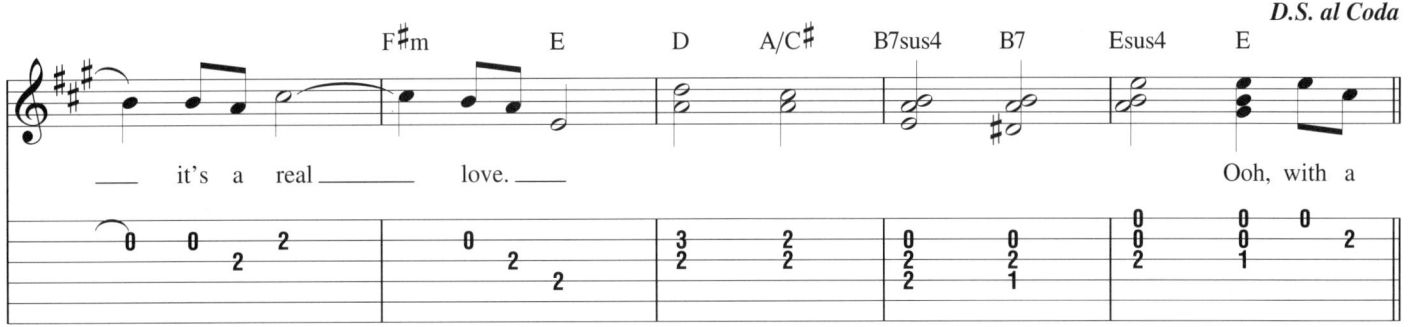
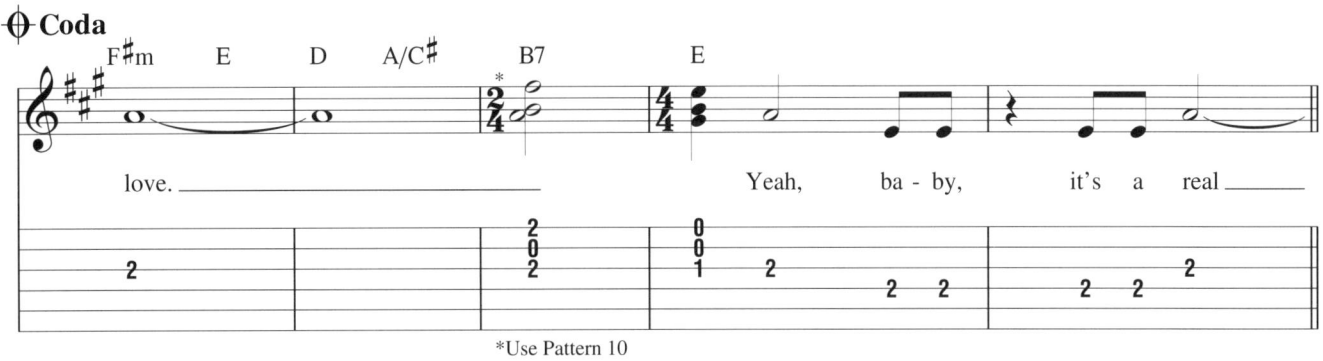
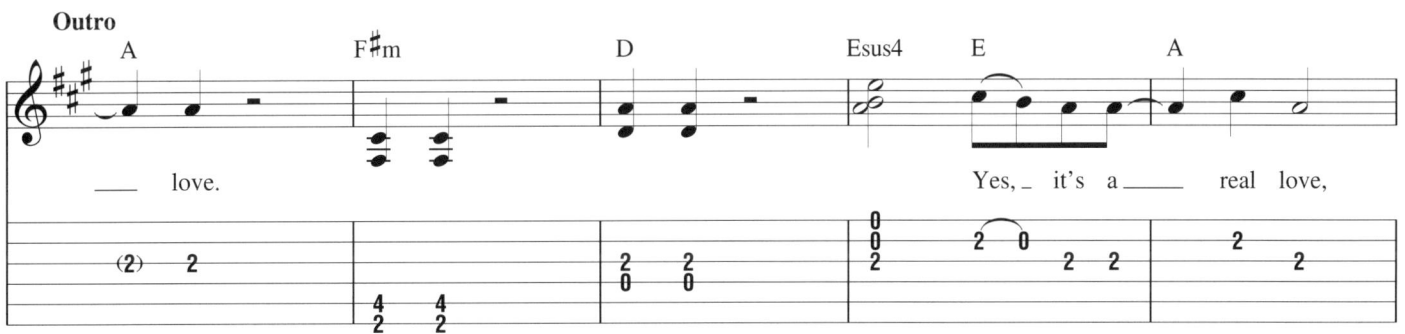
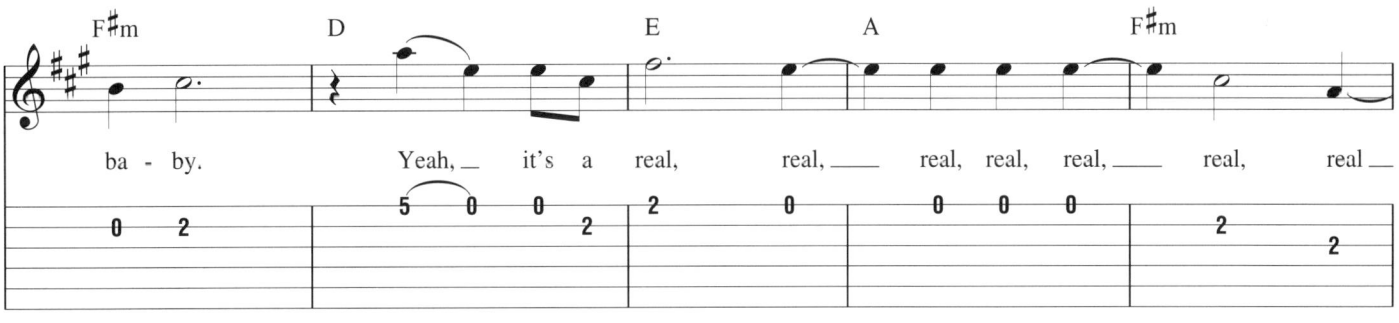
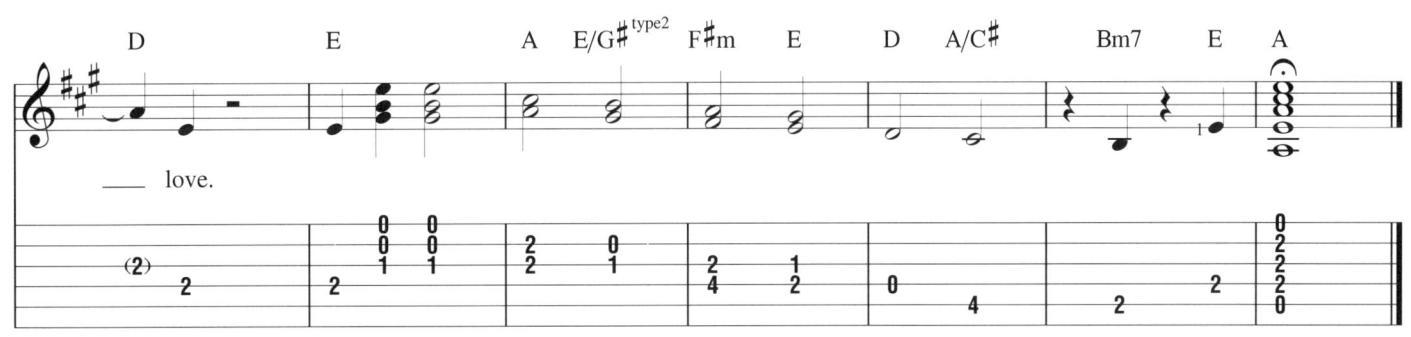

Long Black Train

Words and Music by Josh Turner

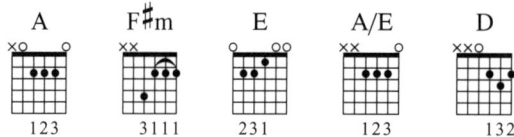

*Capo I

Strum Pattern: 3
Pick Pattern: 4

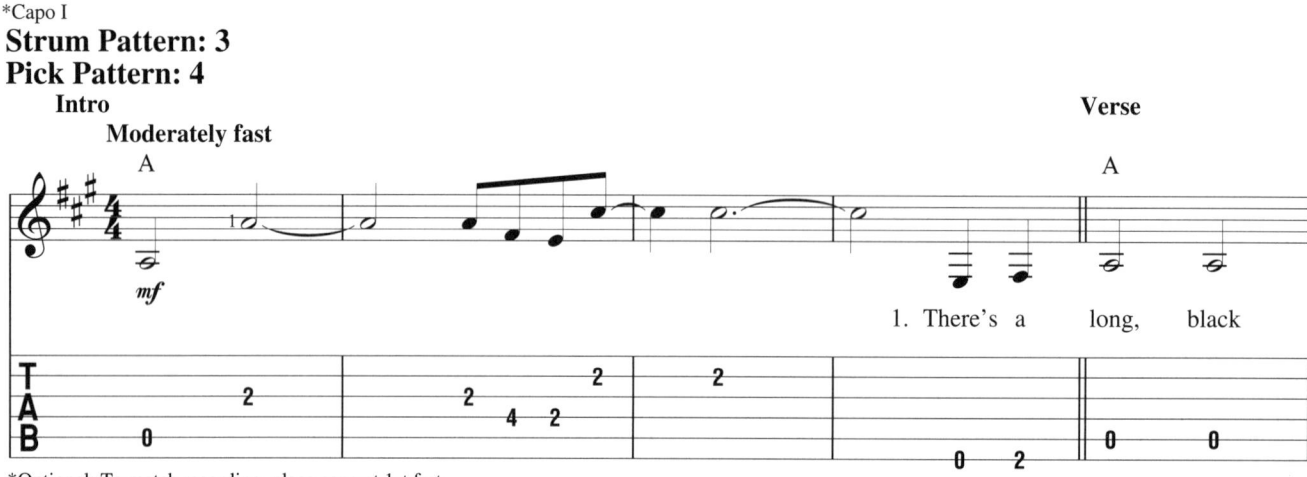

*Optional: To match recording, place capo at 1st fret.

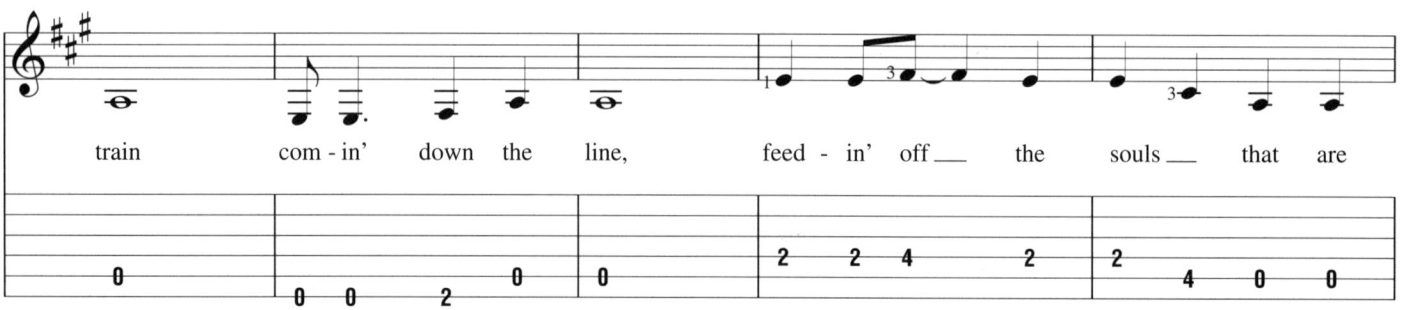

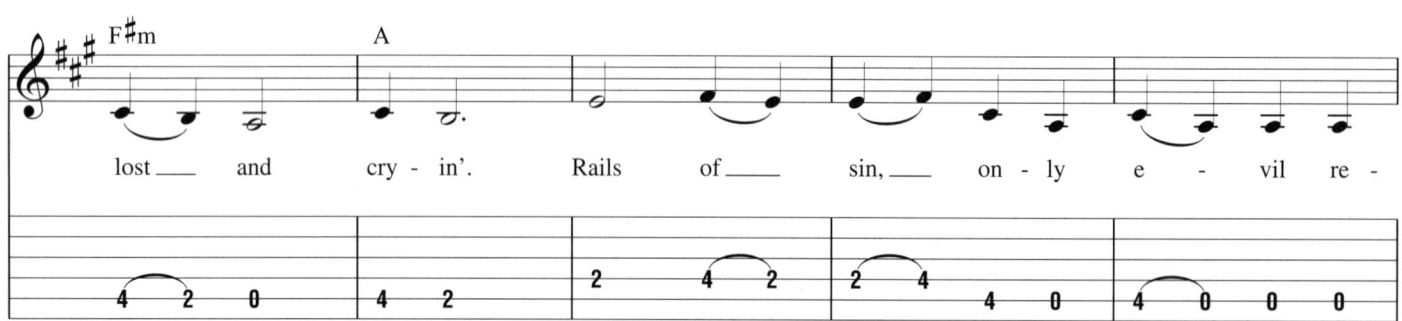

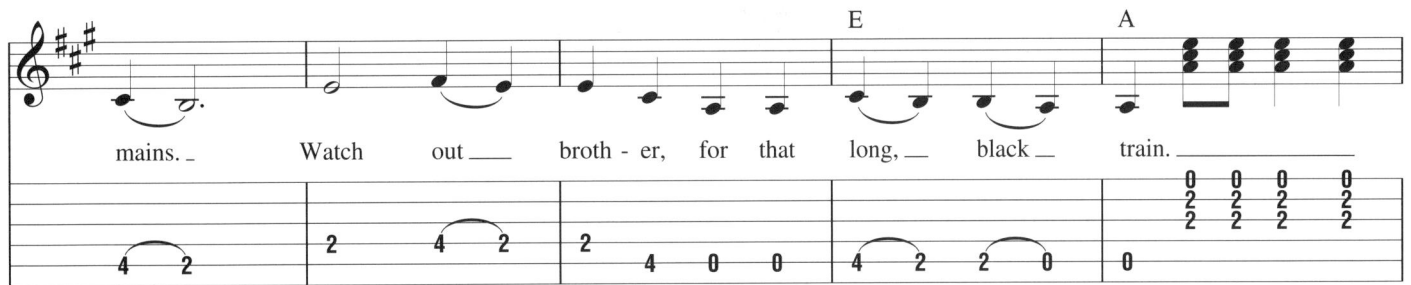
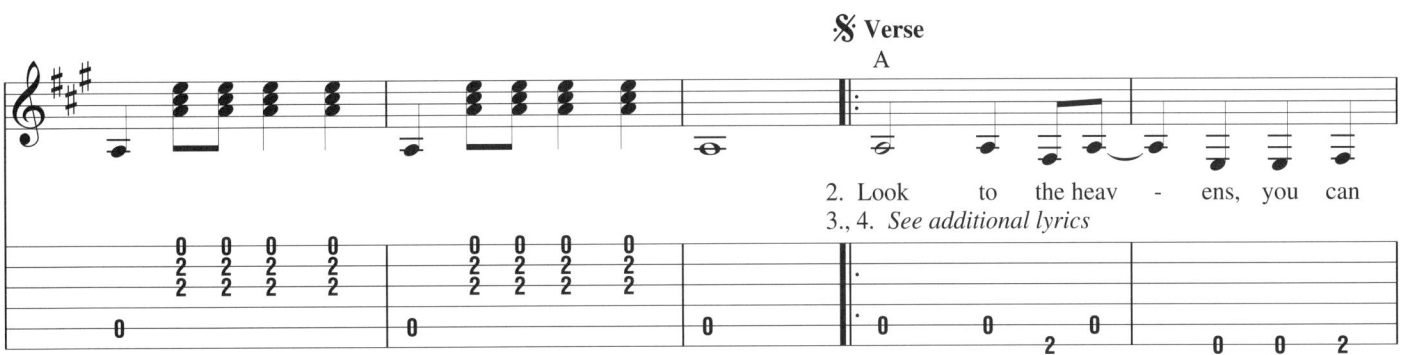

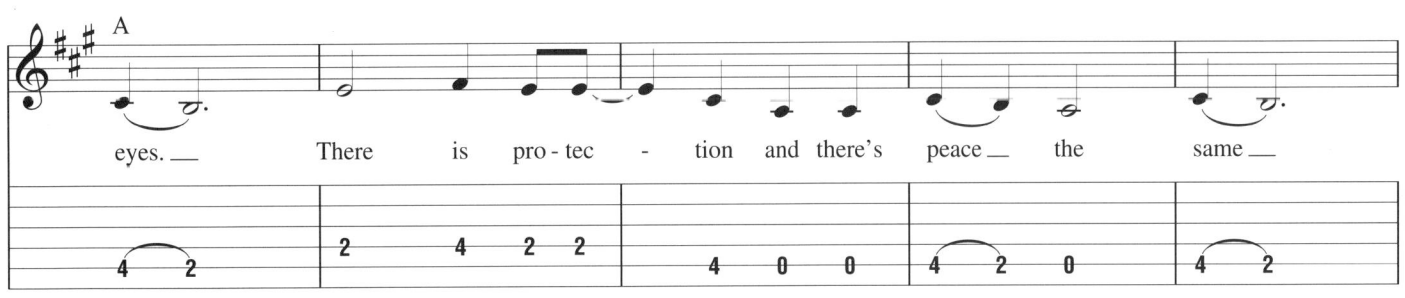
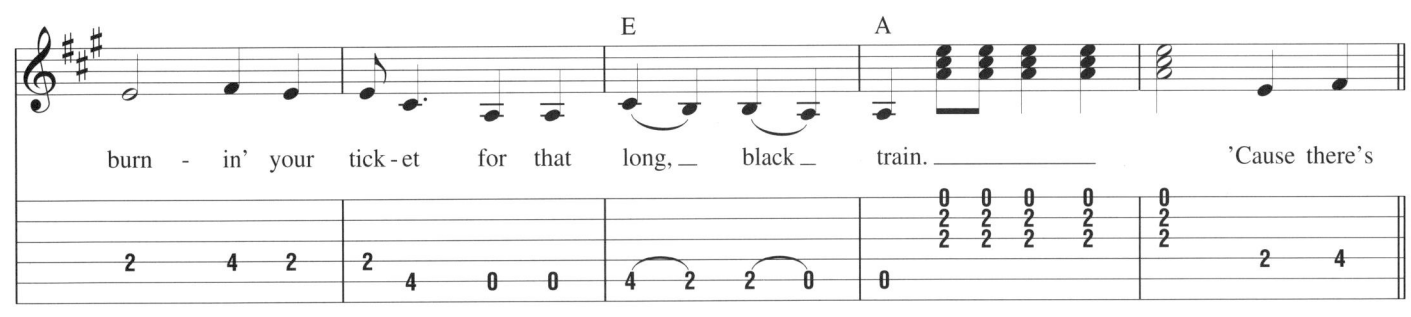

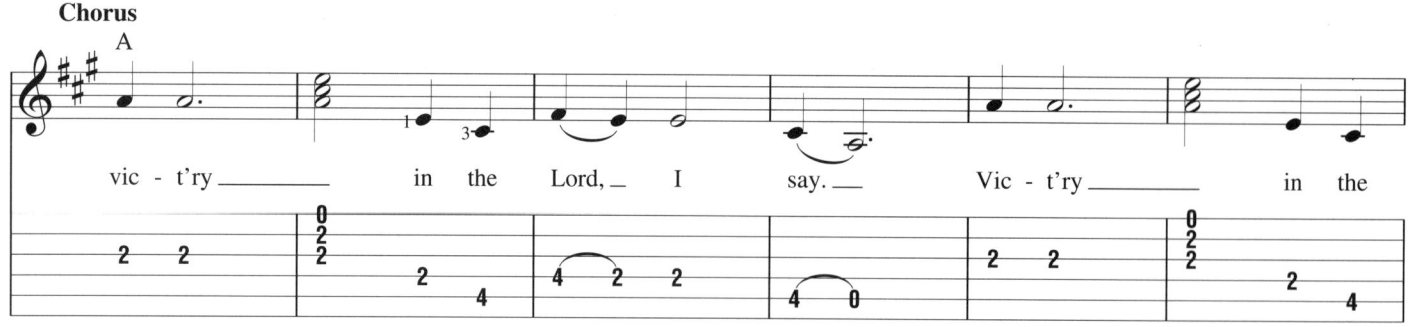
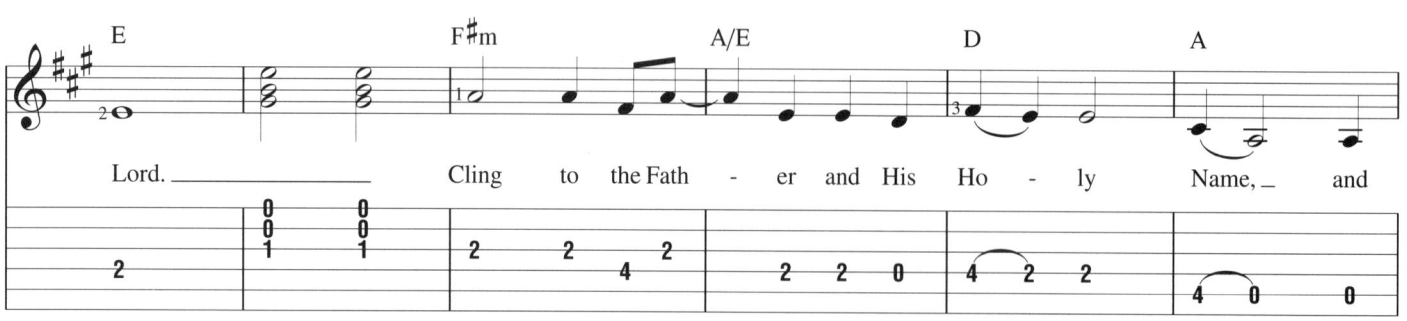
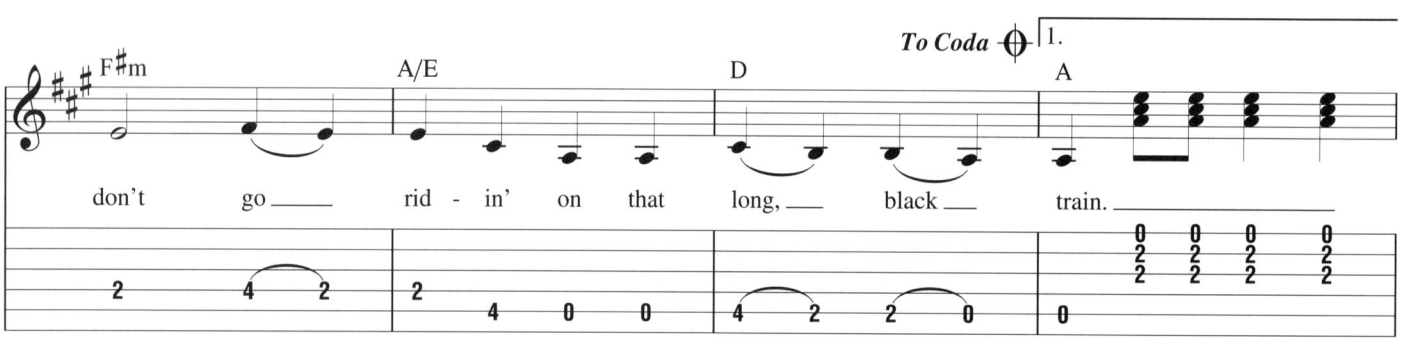
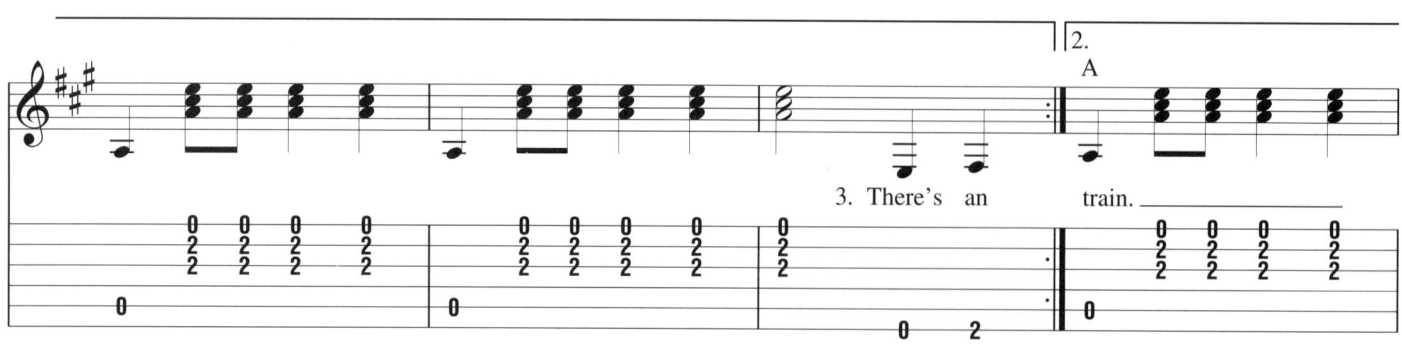
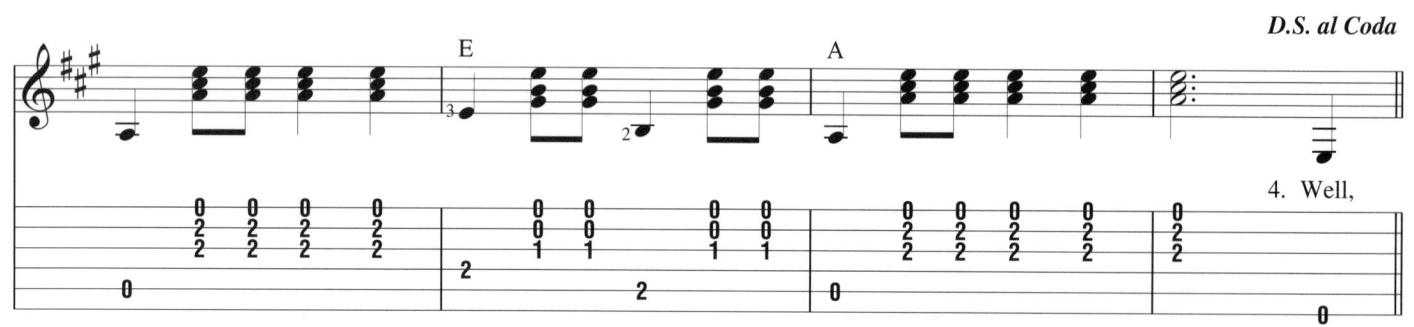

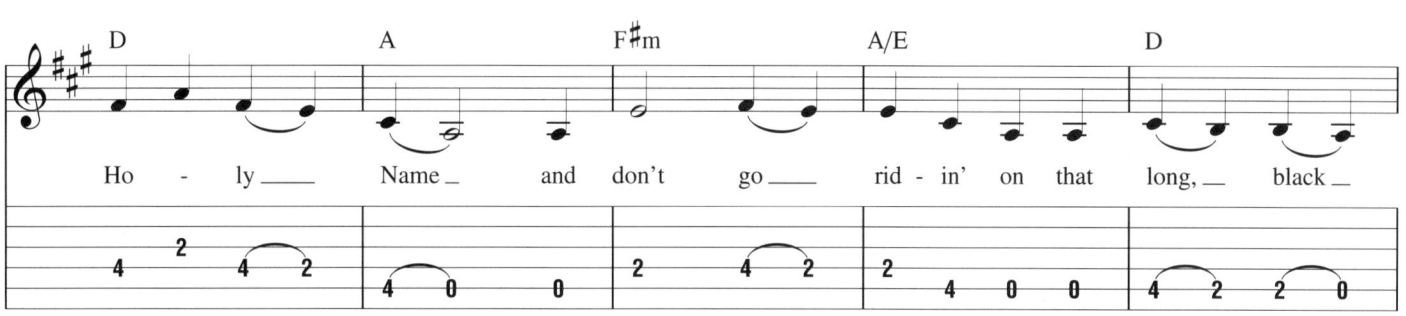
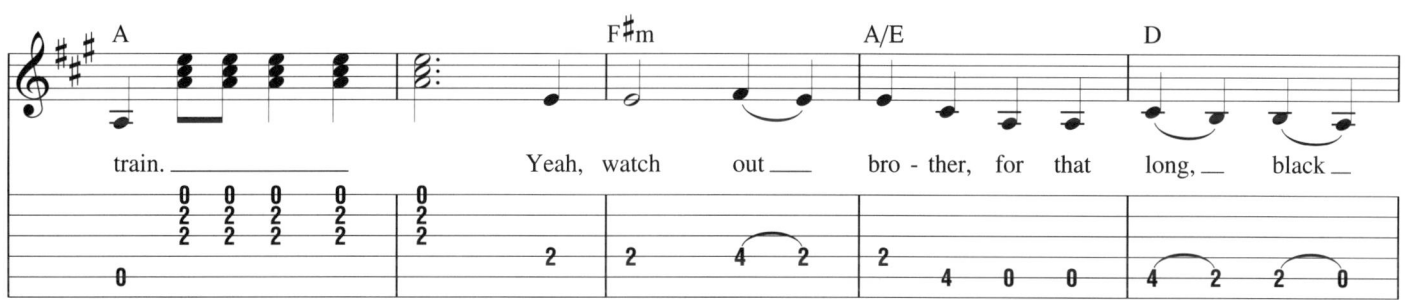
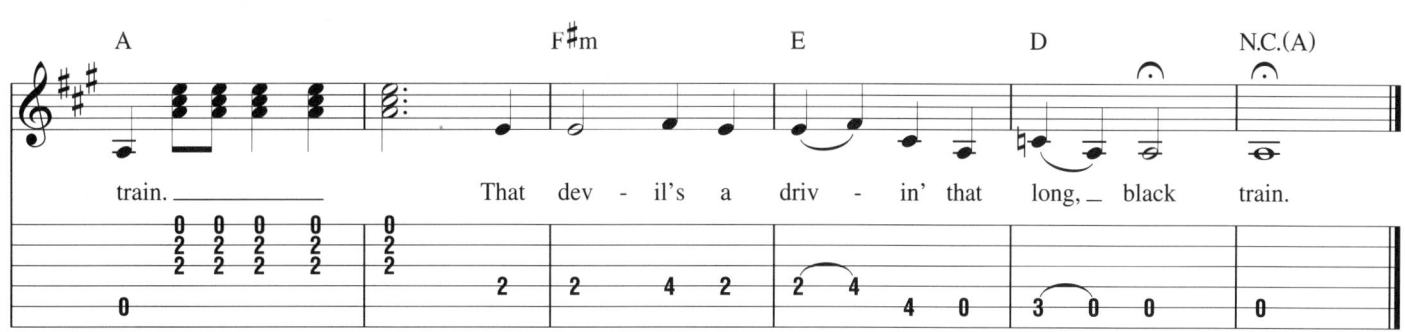

Additional Lyrics

3. There's an engineer on that long, black train,
   Makin' you wonder if the ride is worth the pain.
   He's just a waitin' on your heart to say,
   "Let me ride on that long, black train."
   But, you know there's...

4. Well, I can hear the whistle from a mile away.
   It sounds so good, but I must stay away.
   That train is a beauty, makin' everybody stare,
   But its only destination is the middle of nowhere.
   But, you know there's...

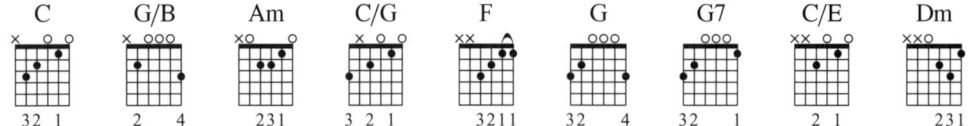

Mud on the Tires

Words and Music by Brad Paisley and Chris Dubois

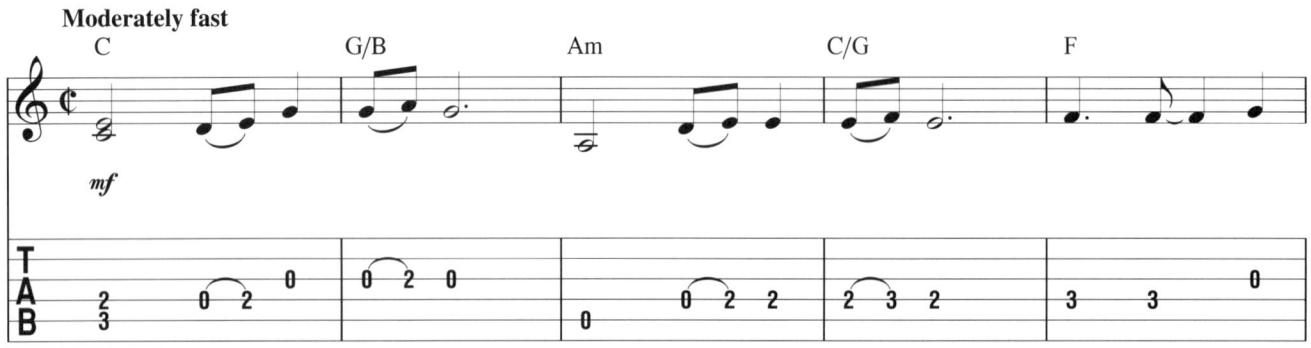

*Capo II
Strum Pattern: 1
Pick Pattern: 3

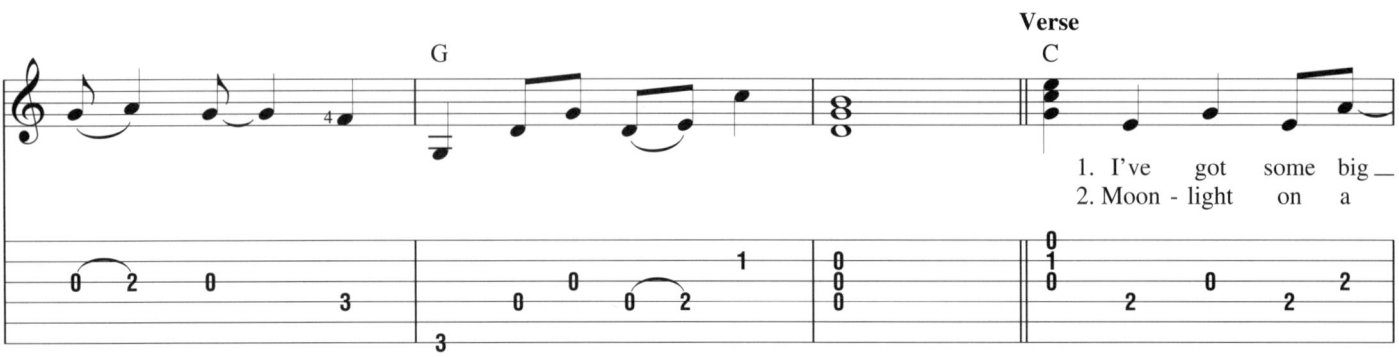

*Optional: To match recording, place capo at 2nd fret.

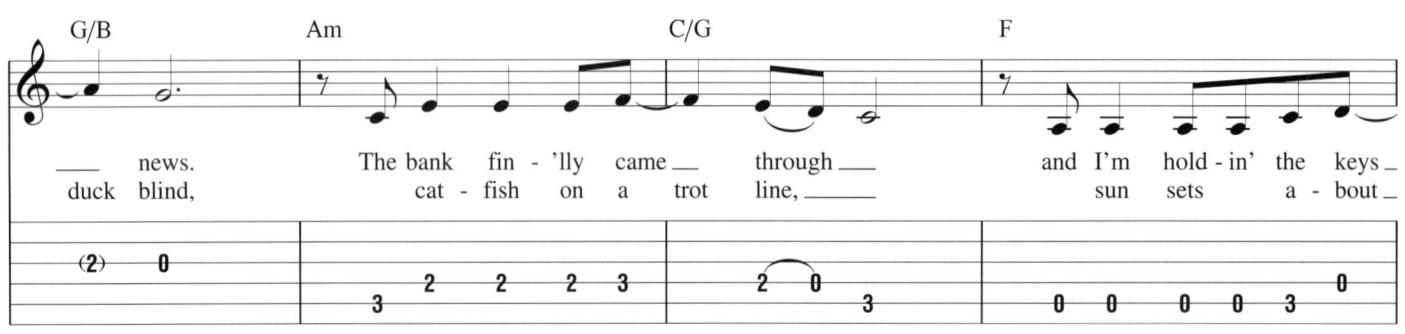

© 2003 EMI APRIL MUSIC INC. and SEA GAYLE MUSIC
All Rights Controlled and Administered by EMI APRIL MUSIC INC.
All Rights Reserved   International Copyright Secured   Used by Permission

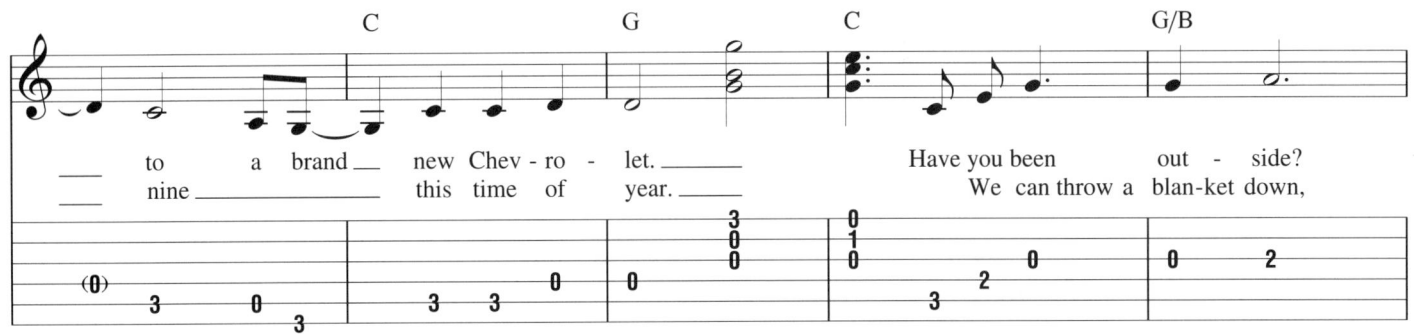
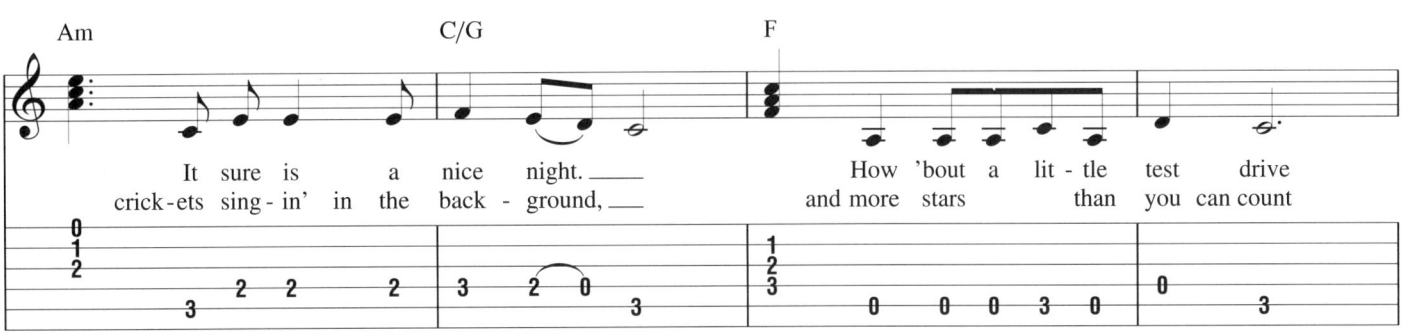

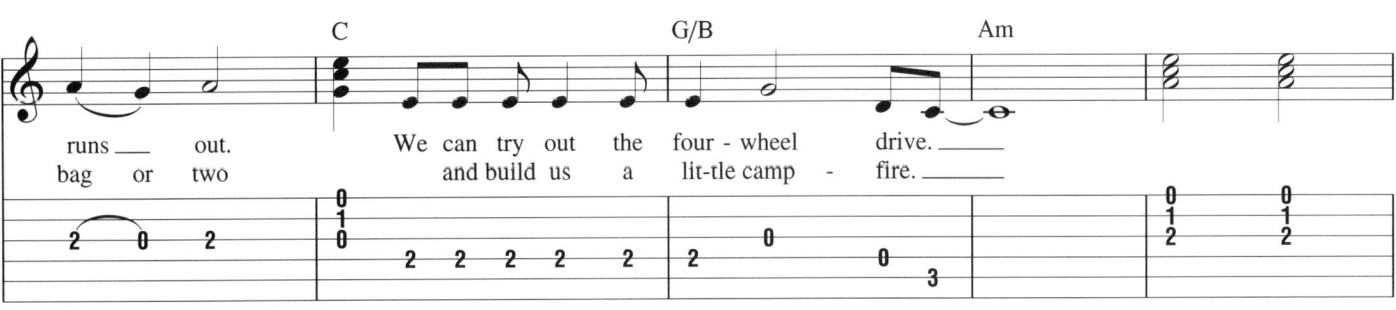

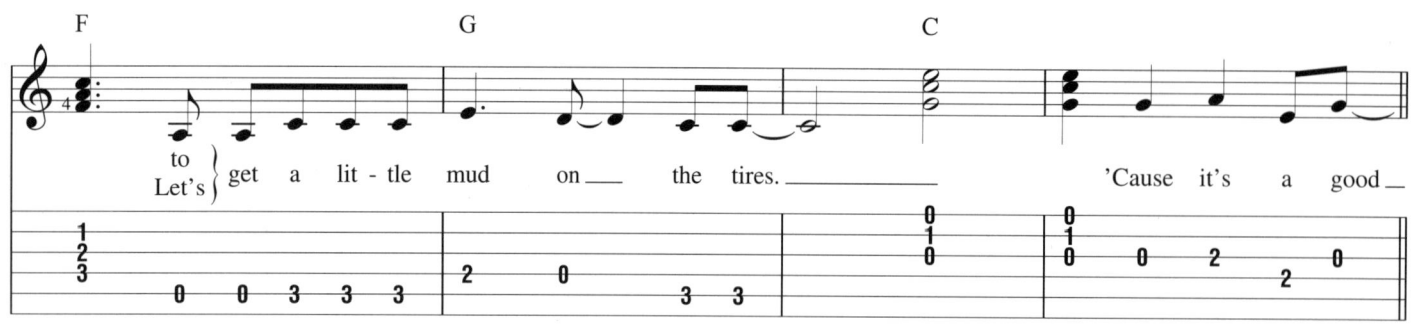
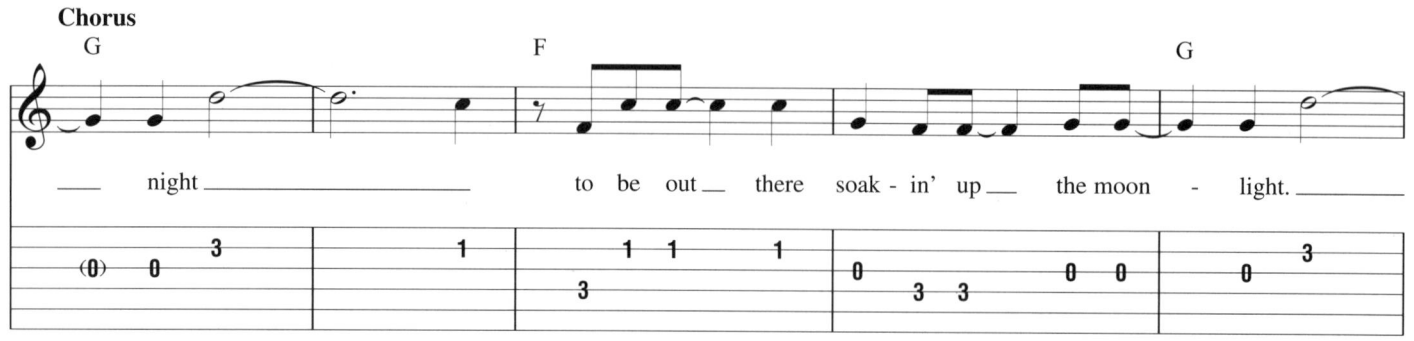
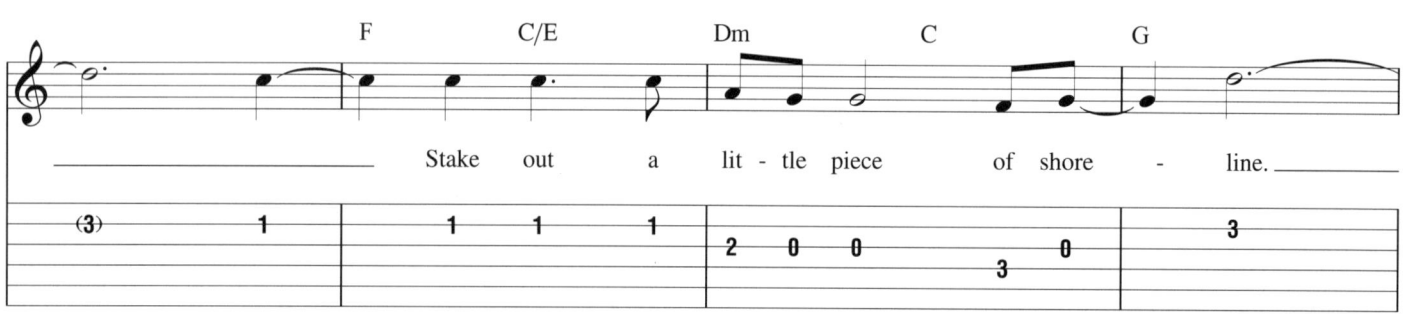
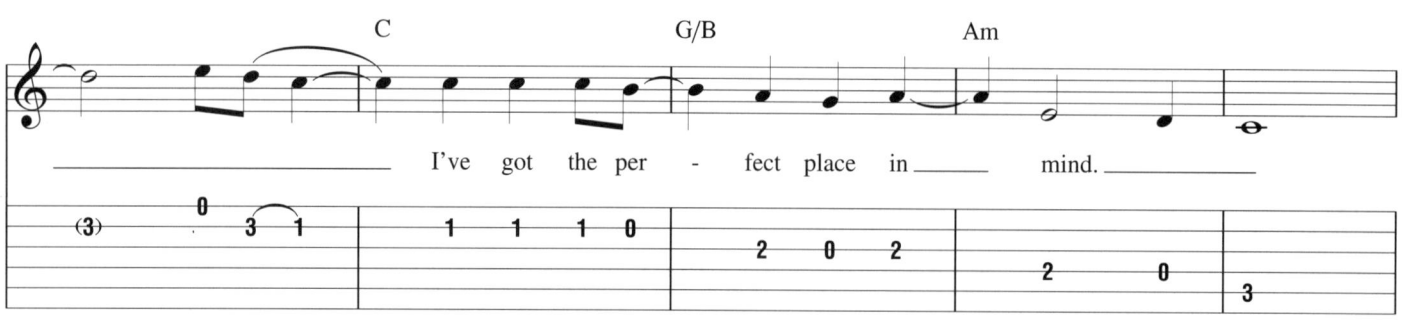
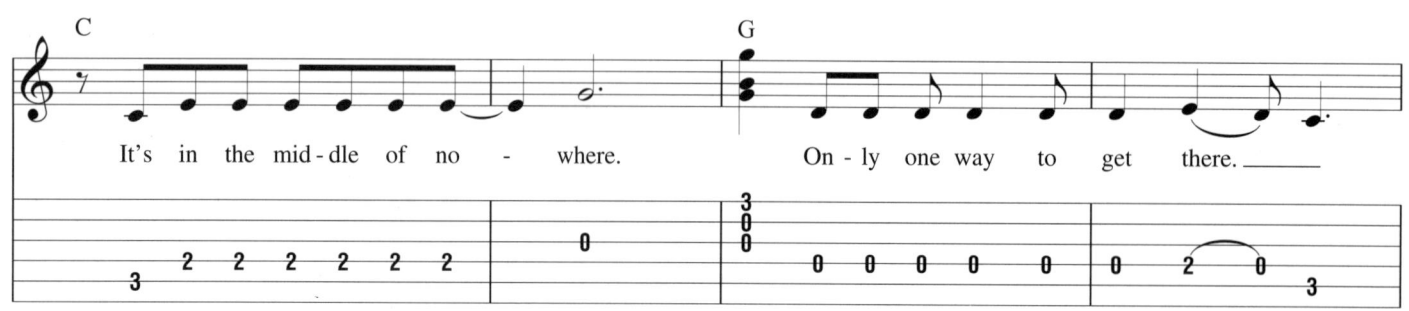

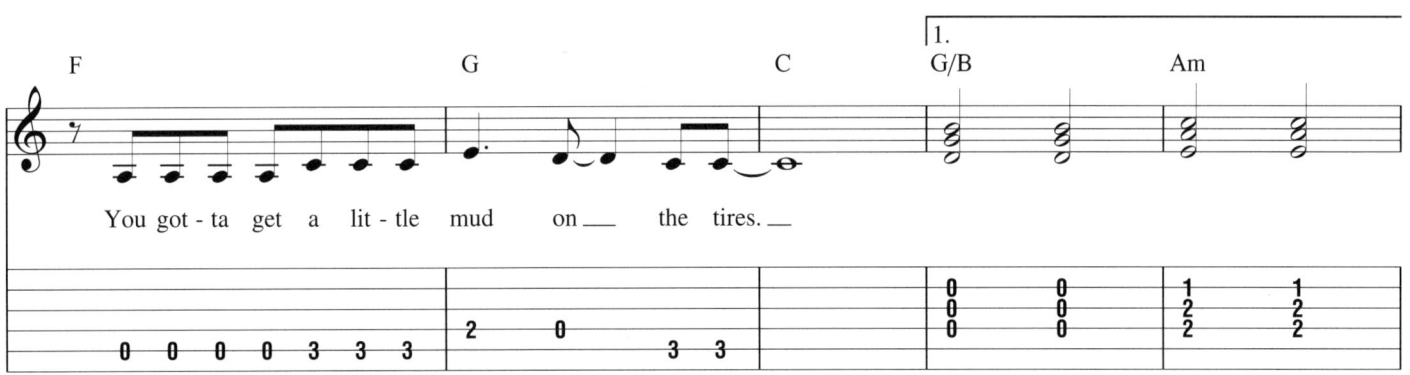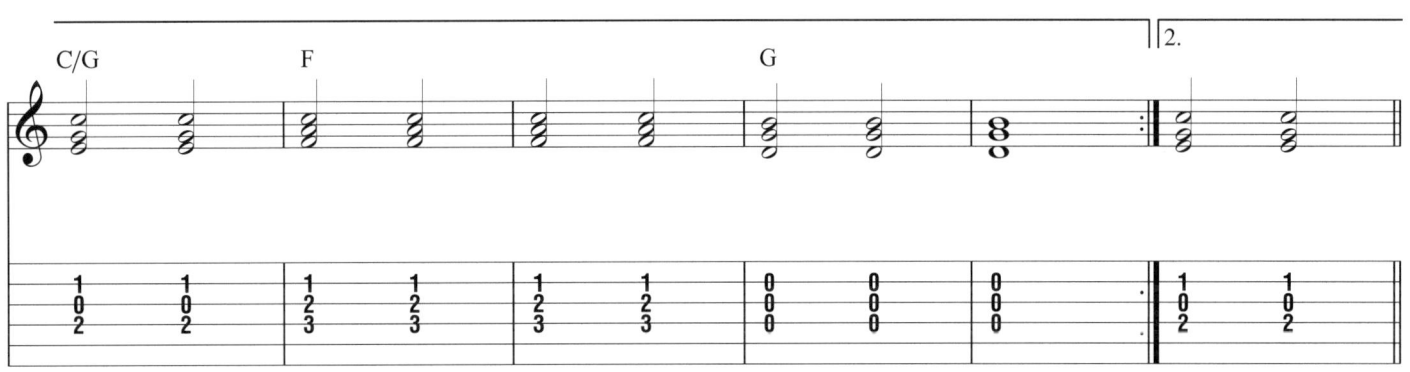

Redneck Woman

Words and Music by Gretchen Wilson and John Rich

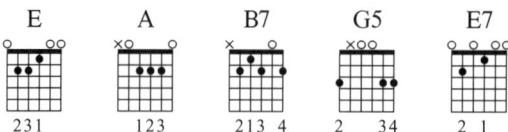

*Capo II
Strum Pattern: 3
Pick Pattern: 4

Intro
Moderately fast

*Optional: To match recording, place capo at 2nd fret.

Verse

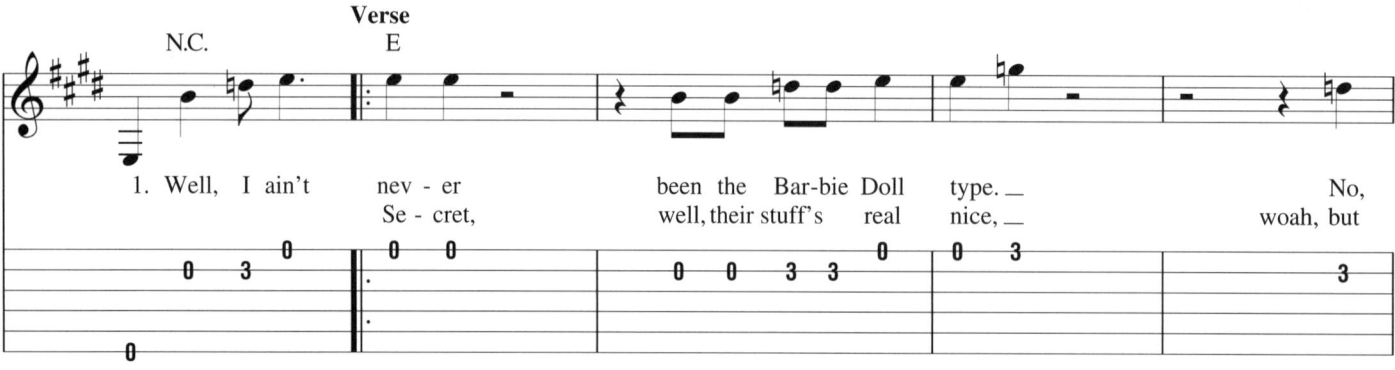

1. Well, I ain't nev-er been the Bar-bie Doll type. No,
   Se-cret, well, their stuff's real nice, woah, but

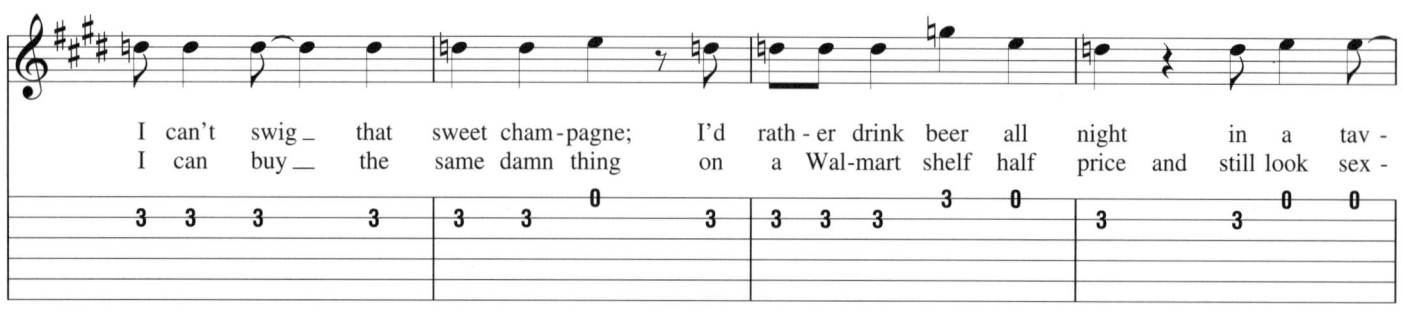

I can't swig that sweet cham-pagne; I'd rath-er drink beer all night in a tav-
I can buy the same damn thing on a Wal-mart shelf half price and still look sex-

Copyright © 2004 Sony/ATV Tunes LLC, Hoosiermama Music and WB Music Corp.
All Rights on behalf of Sony/ATV Tunes LLC and Hoosiermama Music Administered by
Sony/ATV Music Publishing, 8 Music Square West, Nashville, TN 37203
International Copyright Secured   All Rights Reserved

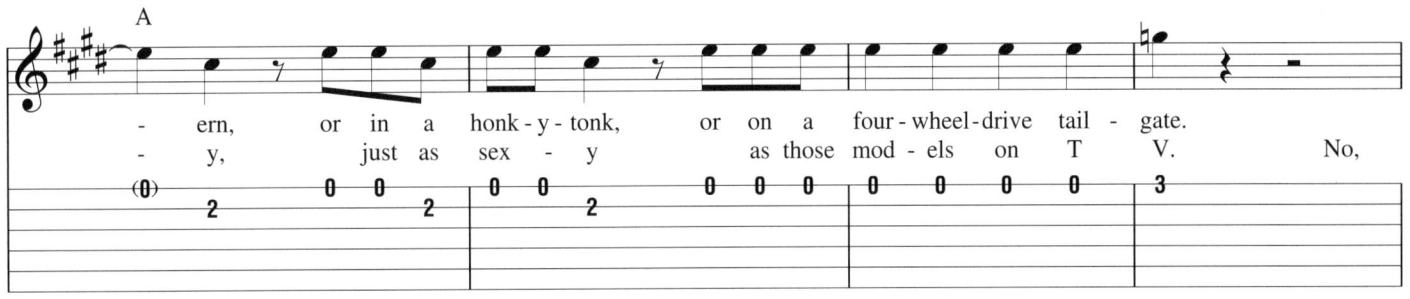

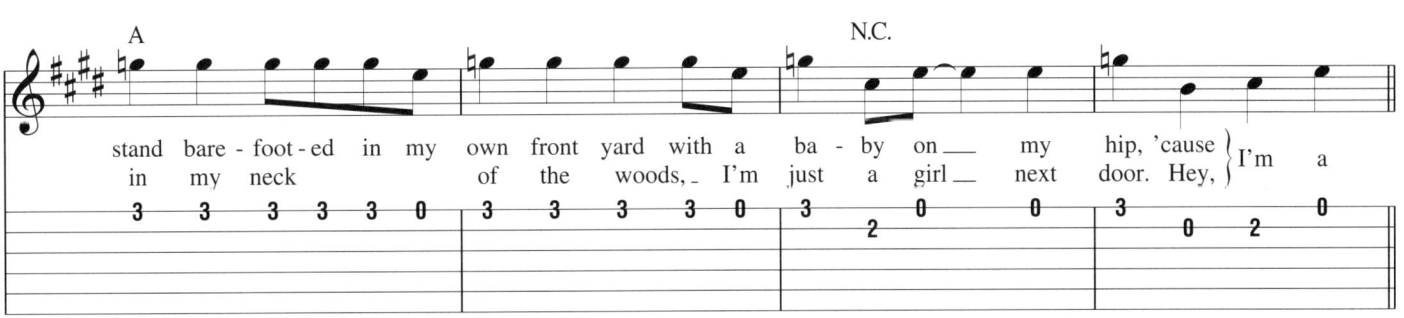

Chorus

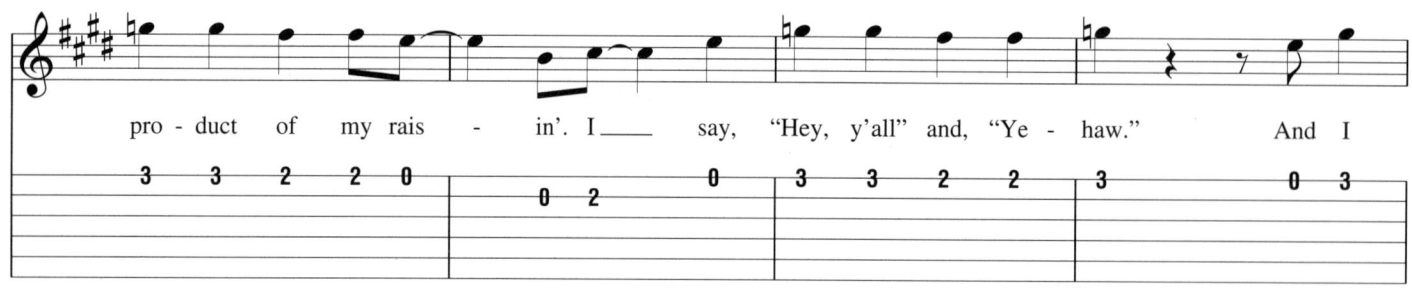
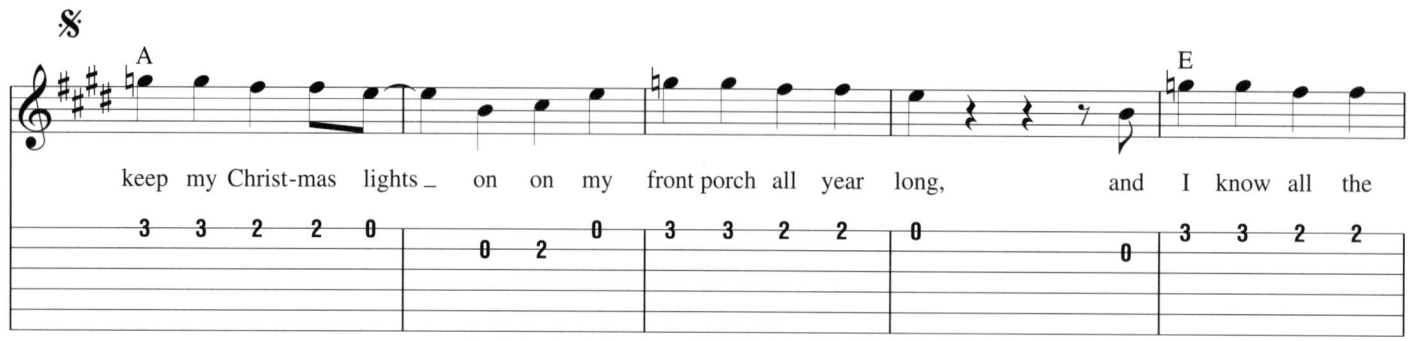
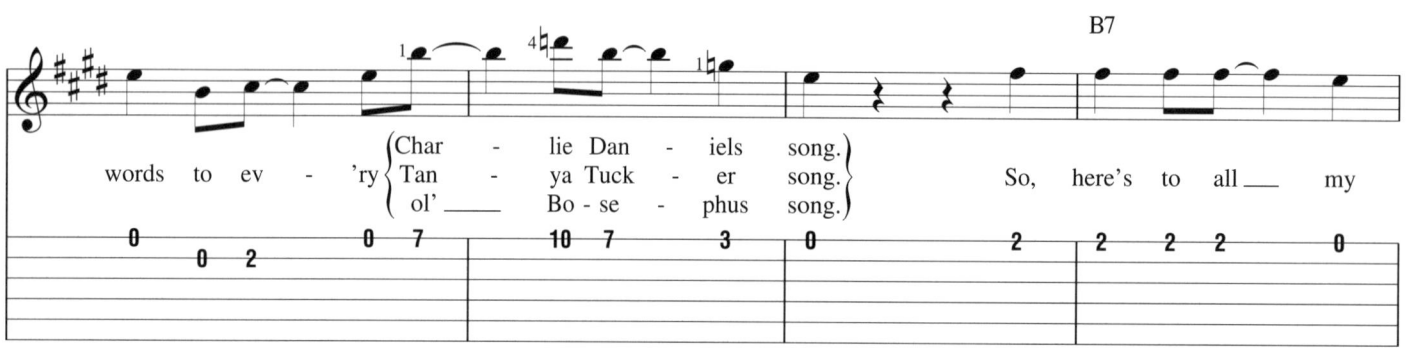

*1st & 3rd times

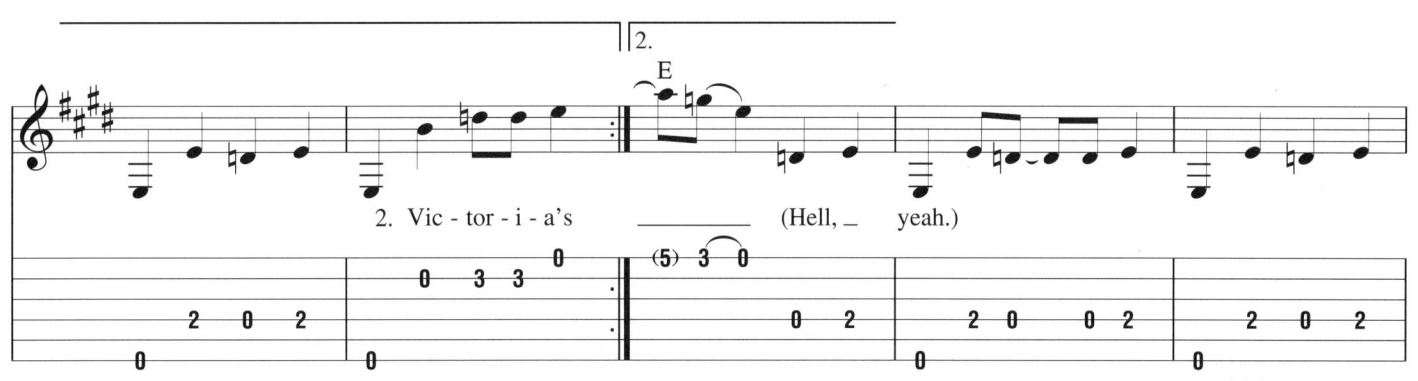
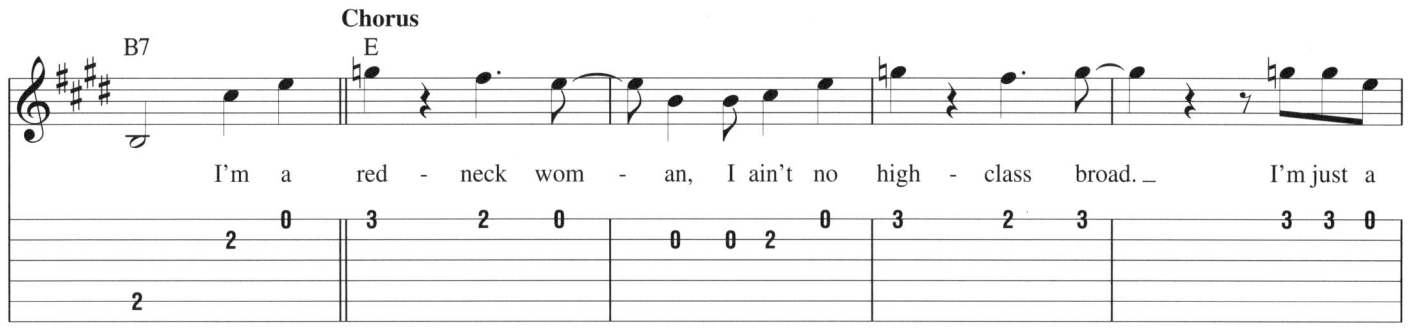
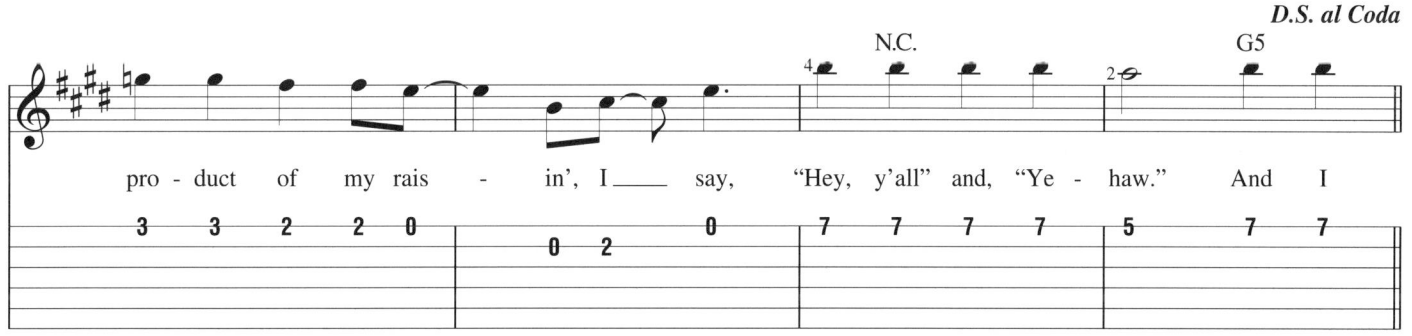

Remember When

Words and Music by Alan Jackson

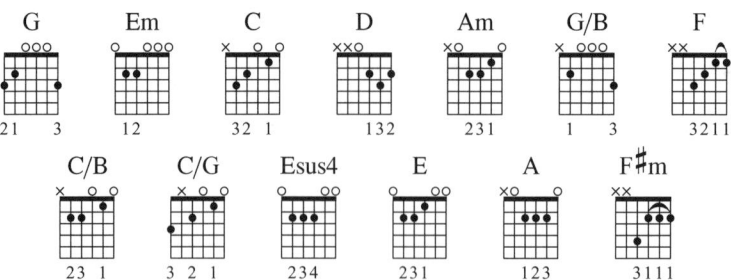

Strum Pattern: 1, 3
Pick Pattern: 4, 5

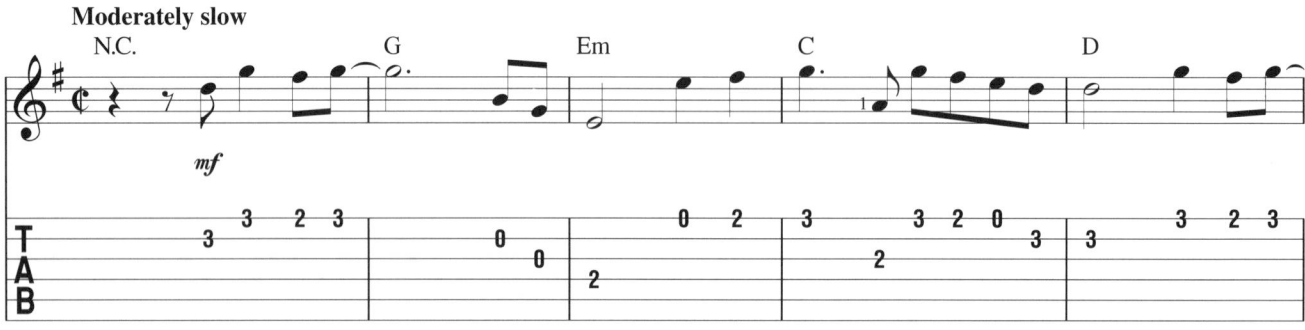

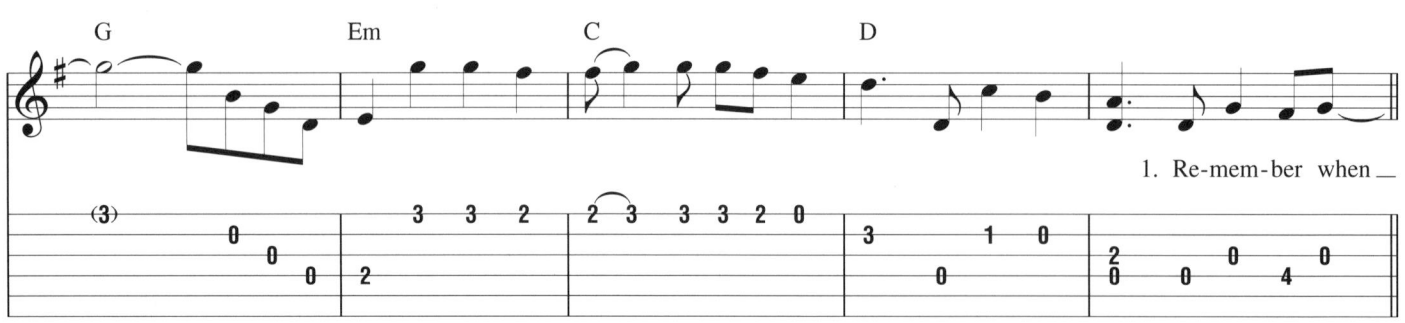

I was young ___ and so were you ___ and time stood still ___
we vowed the vows ___ and walked the walk ___ and gave our hearts ___
old ones died ___ and new were born ___ and life was changed, ___

© 2003 EMI APRIL MUSIC INC. and TRI-ANGELS MUSIC
All Rights Controlled and Administered by EMI APRIL MUSIC INC.
All Rights Reserved   International Copyright Secured   Used by Permission

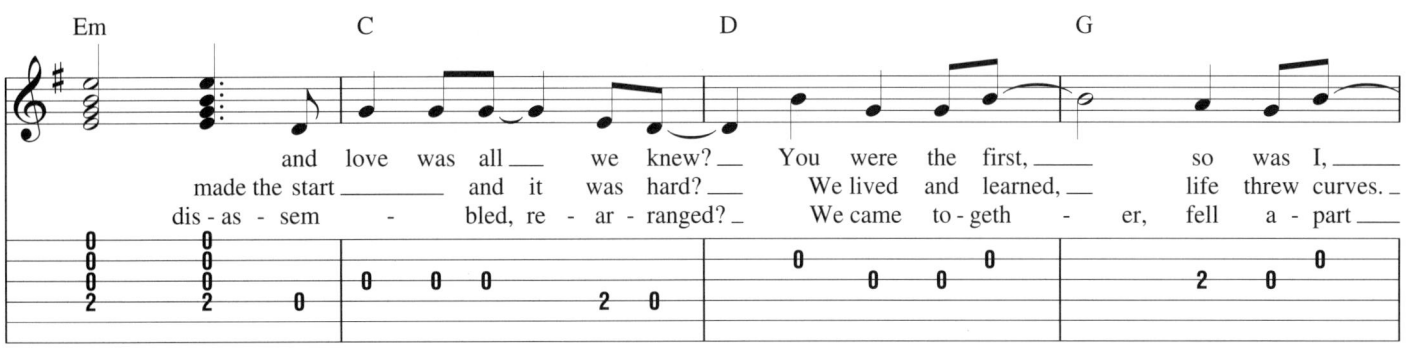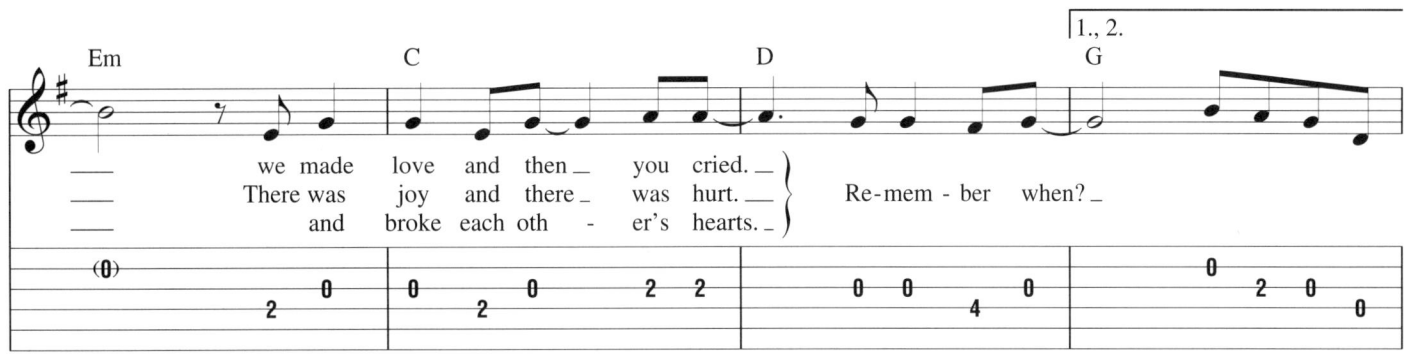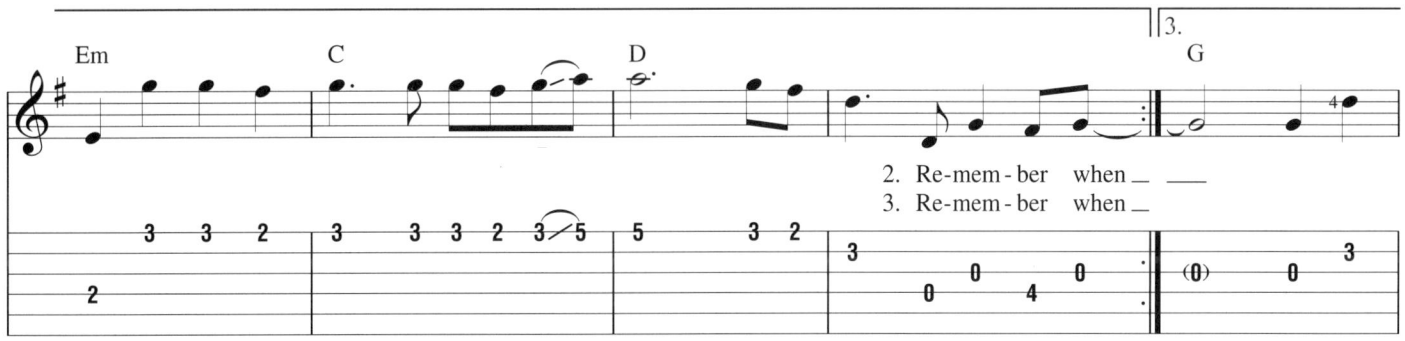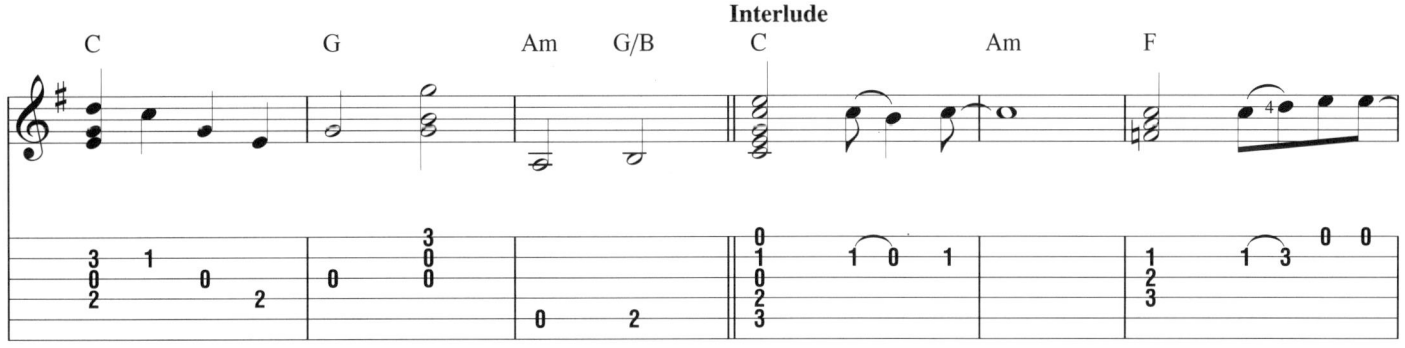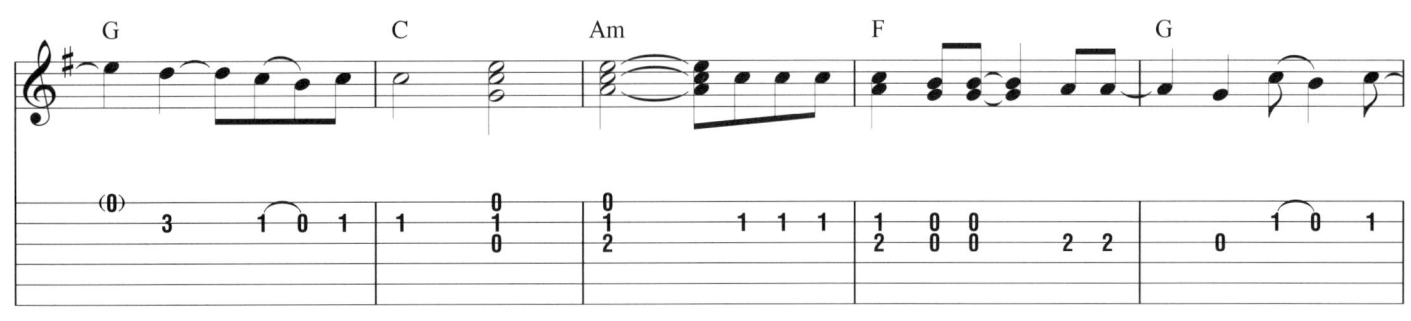

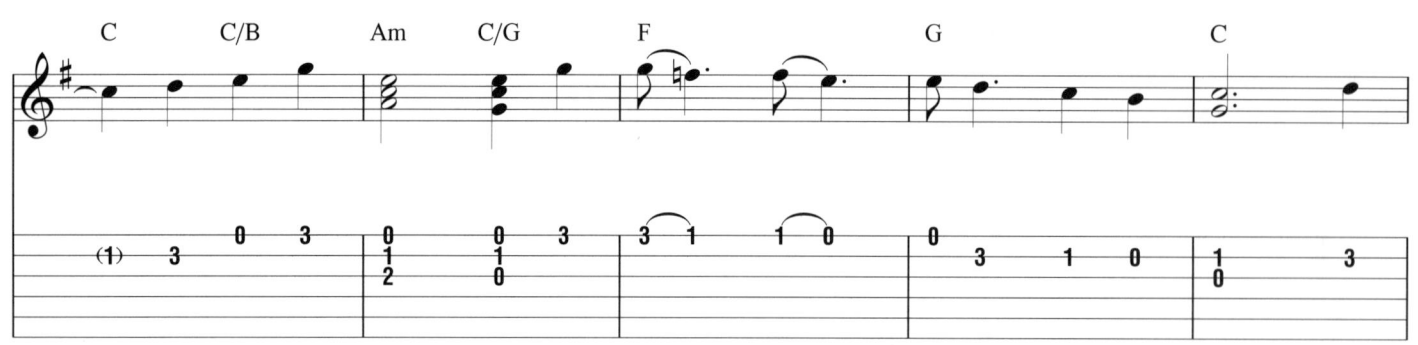
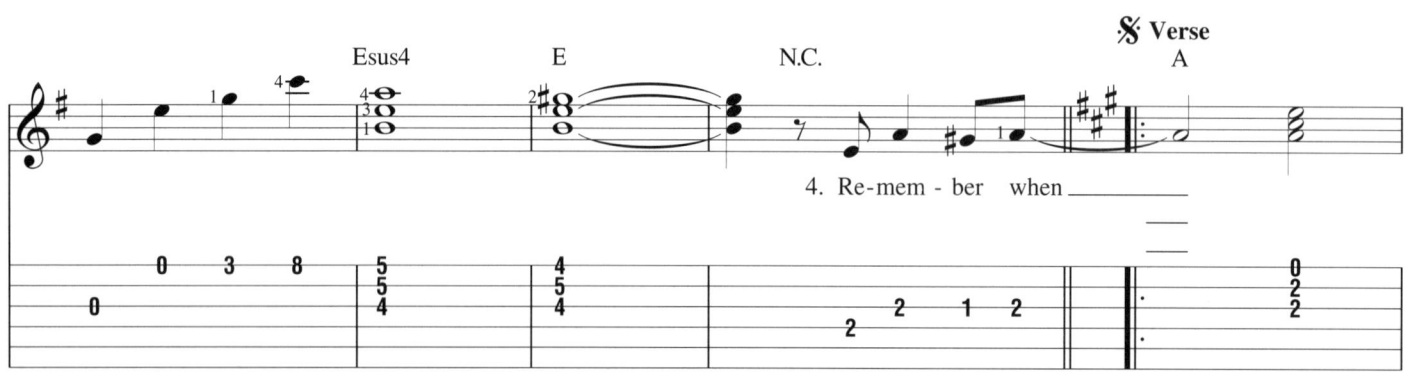
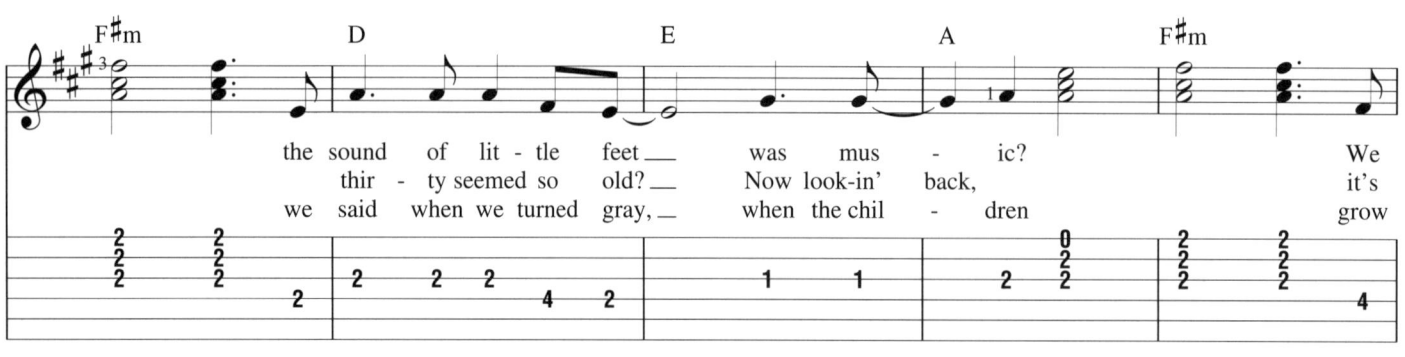
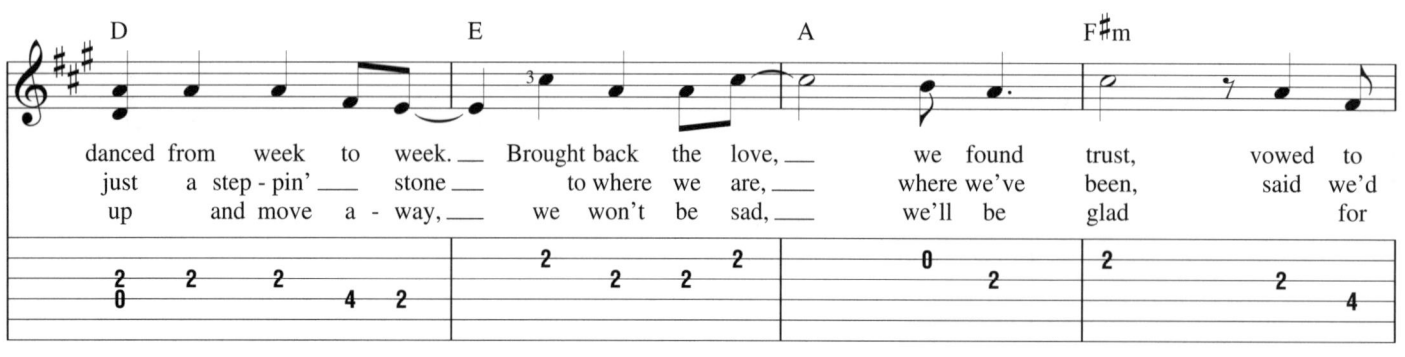

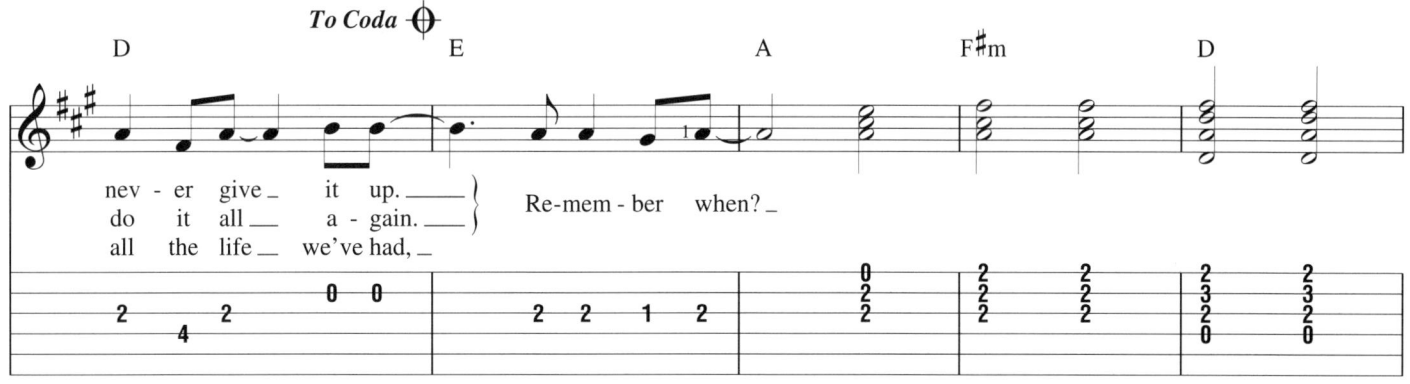
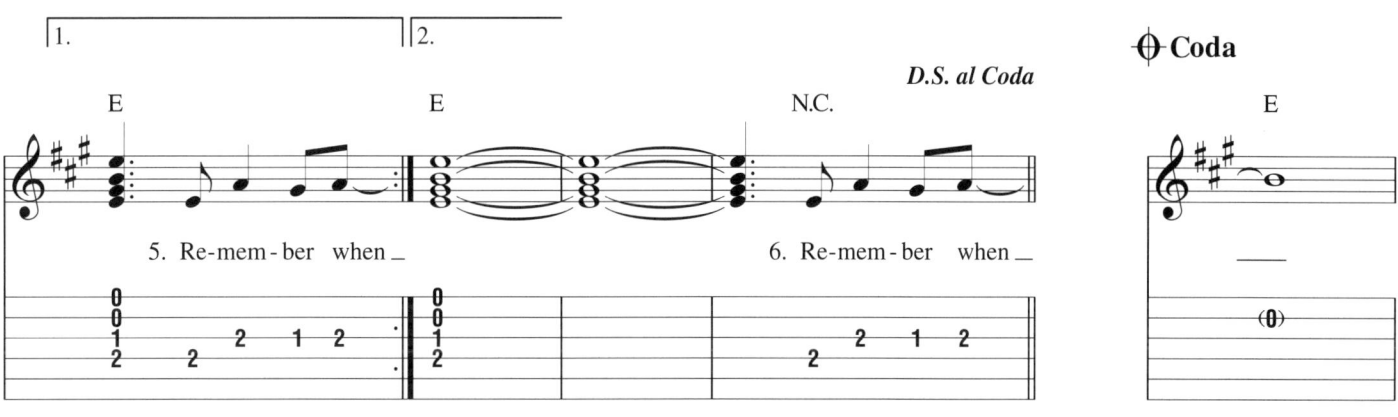

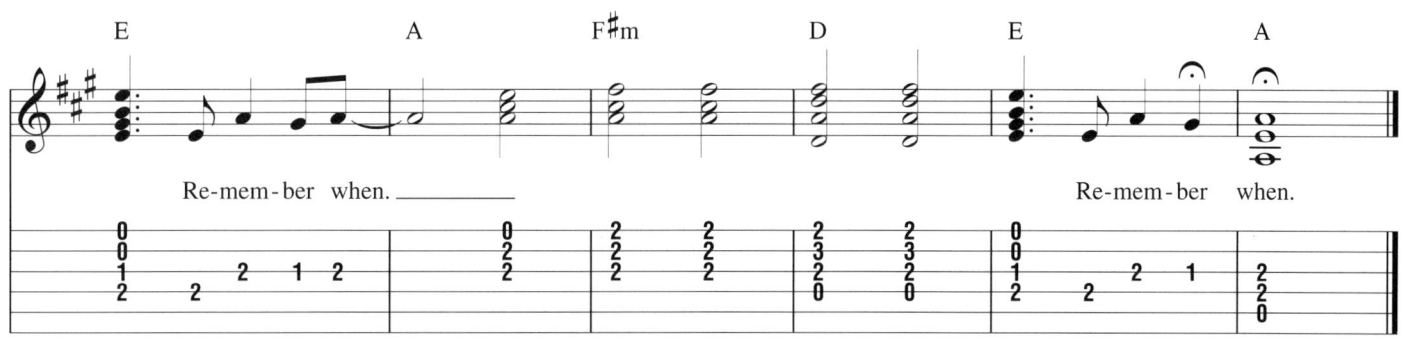

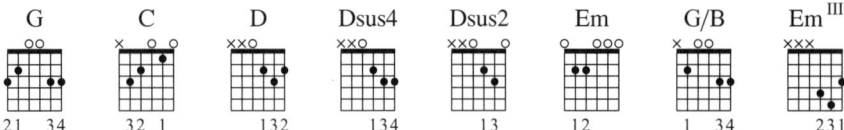

This One's for the Girls

Words and Music by Aimee Mayo, Hillary Lindsey and Chris Lindsey

Chords: G C D Dsus4 Dsus2 Em G/B Em III

*Capo I

Strum Pattern: 1
Pick Pattern: 3

Intro
Moderately

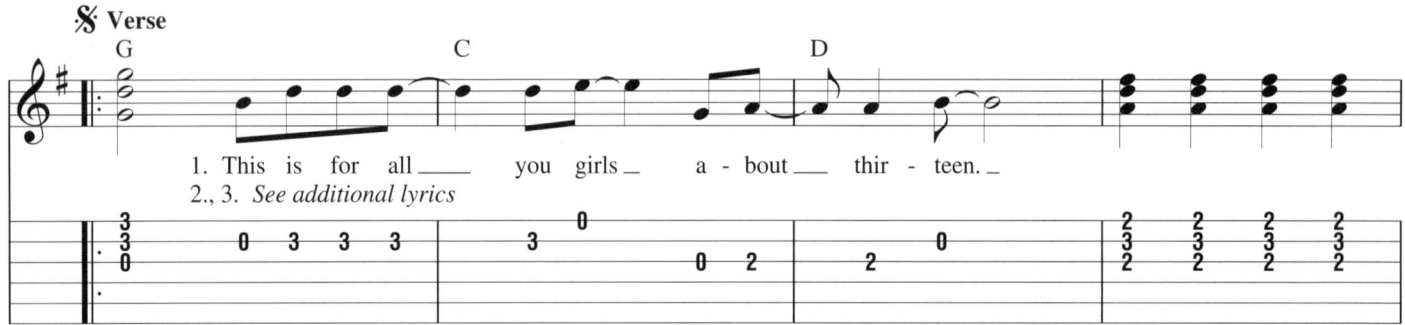

*Optional: To match recording, place capo at 1st fret.

Verse

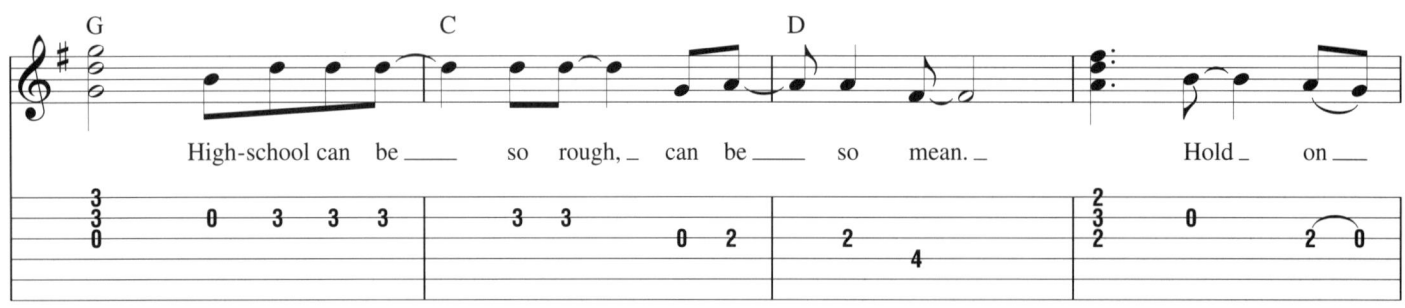

1. This is for all you girls about thirteen.
2., 3. See additional lyrics

High-school can be so rough, can be so mean. Hold on

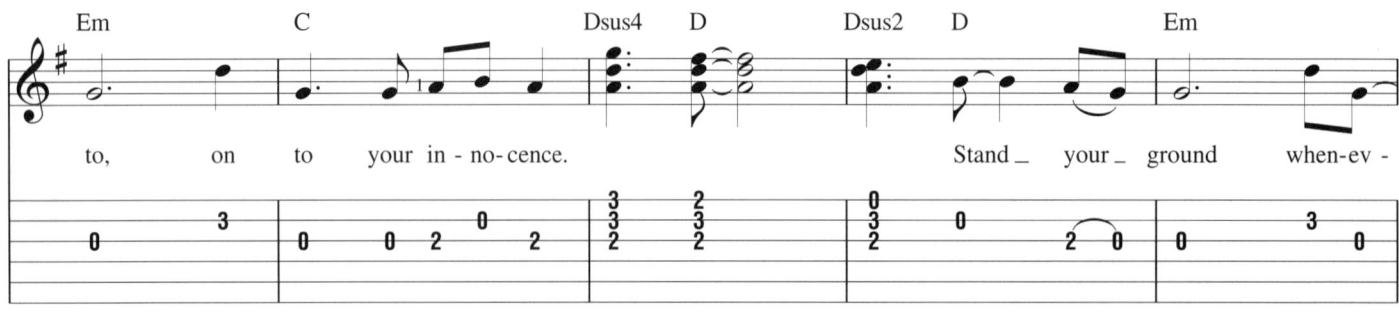

to, on to your in-no-cence. Stand your ground when-ev-

Copyright © 2003 by Careers-BMG Music Publishing, Inc., Silverkiss Music Publishing, Inc.,
Famous Music Corporation, Animal Fair, Nashville DreamWorks Songs and Monkey Feet Music
All Rights for Silverkiss Music Publishing, Inc. Administered by Careers-BMG Music Publishing, Inc.
All Rights for Animal Fair Administered by Famous Music Corporation
All Rights for Nashville DreamWorks Songs and Monkey Feet Music Administered by Cherry Lane Music Publishing Company, Inc.
International Copyright Secured   All Rights Reserved

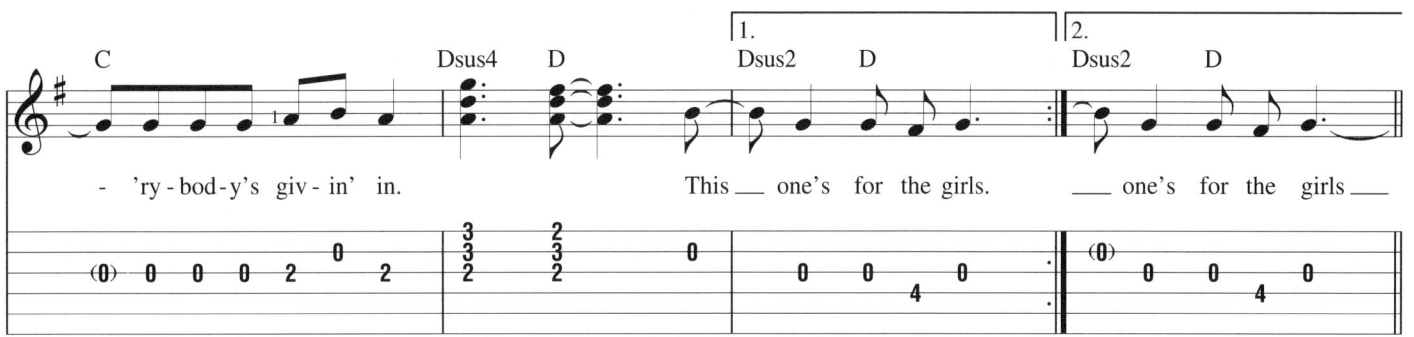
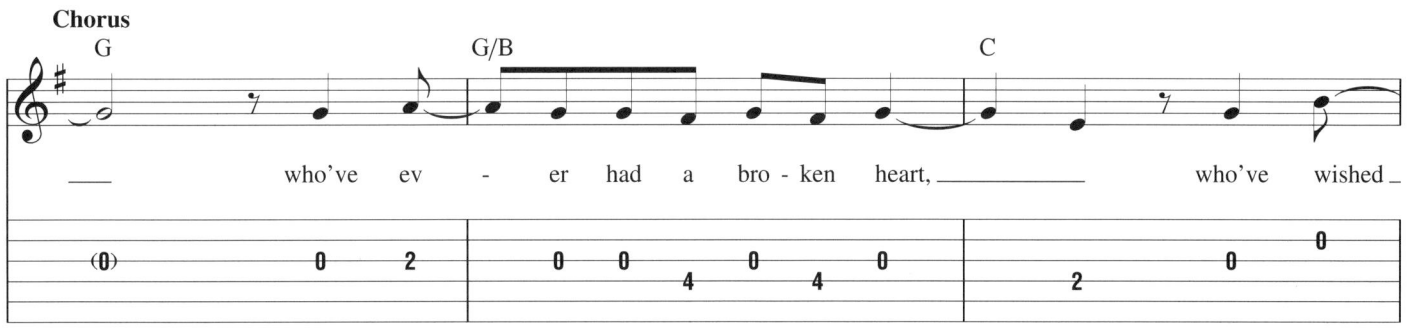

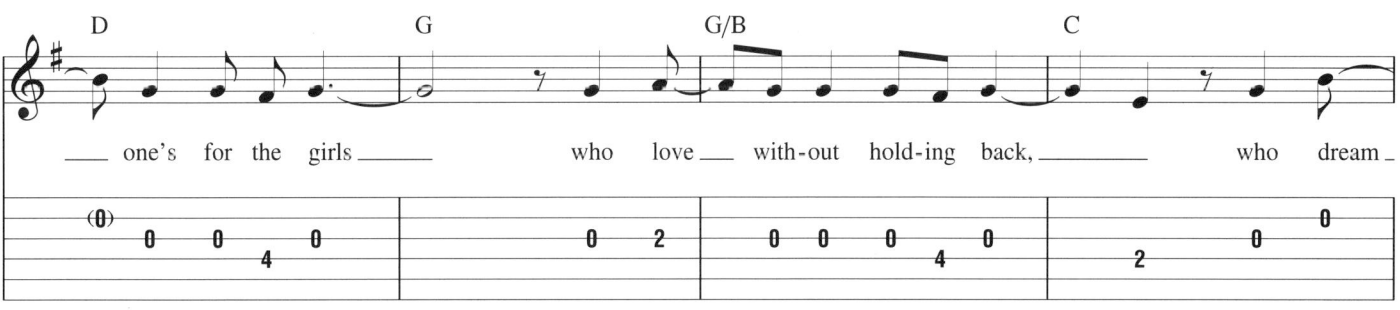
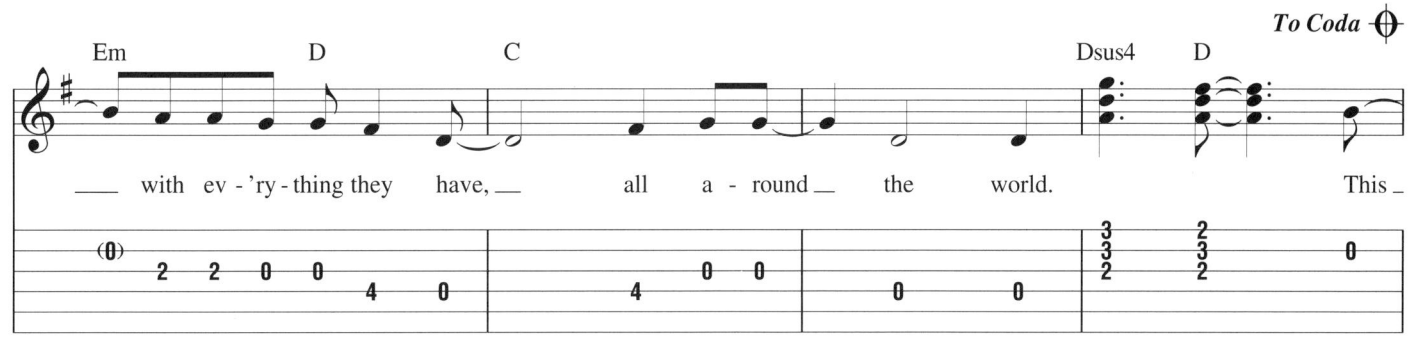

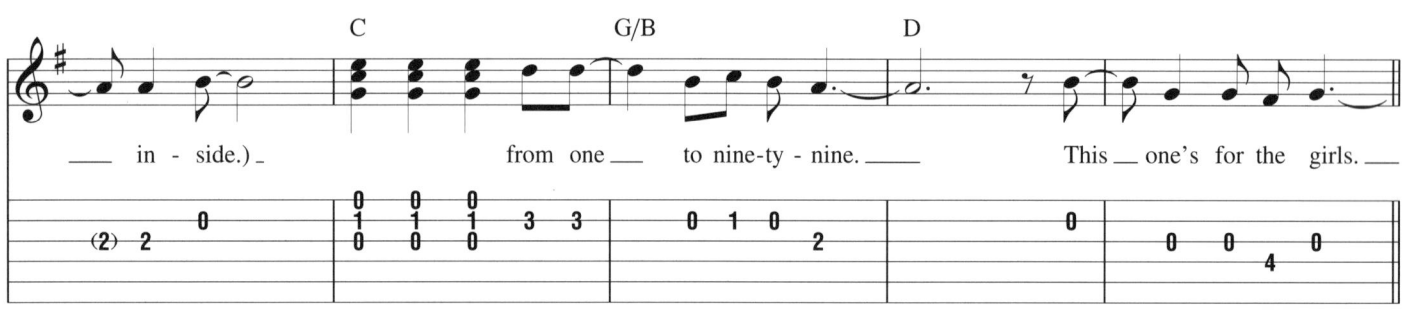
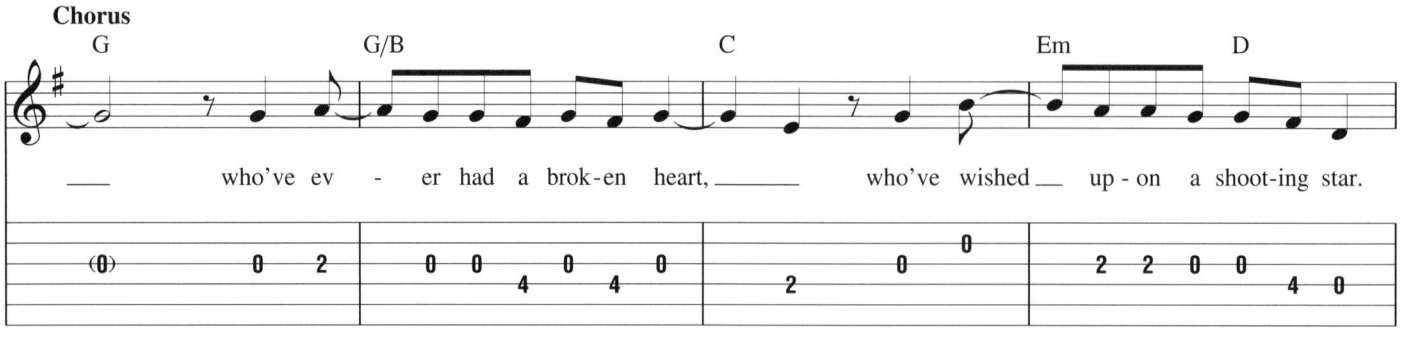
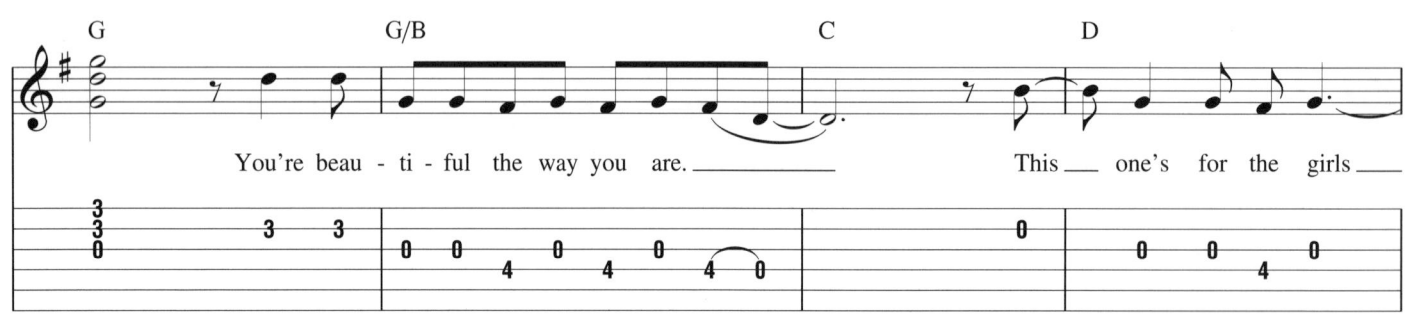

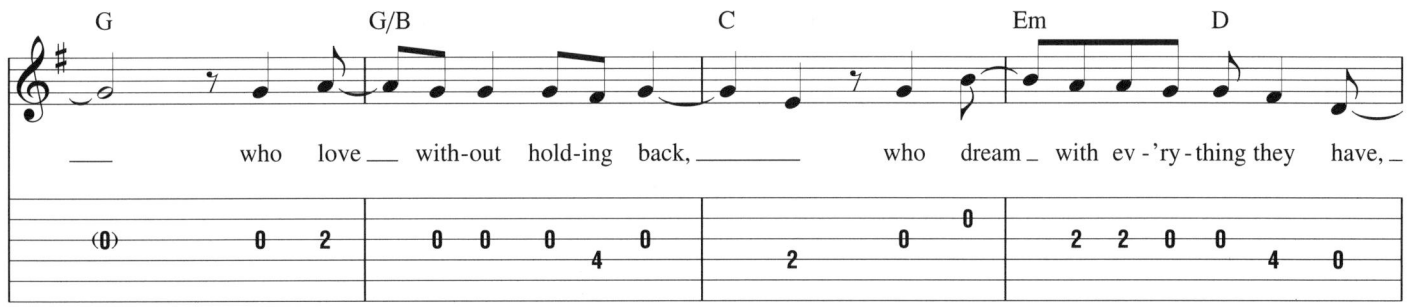

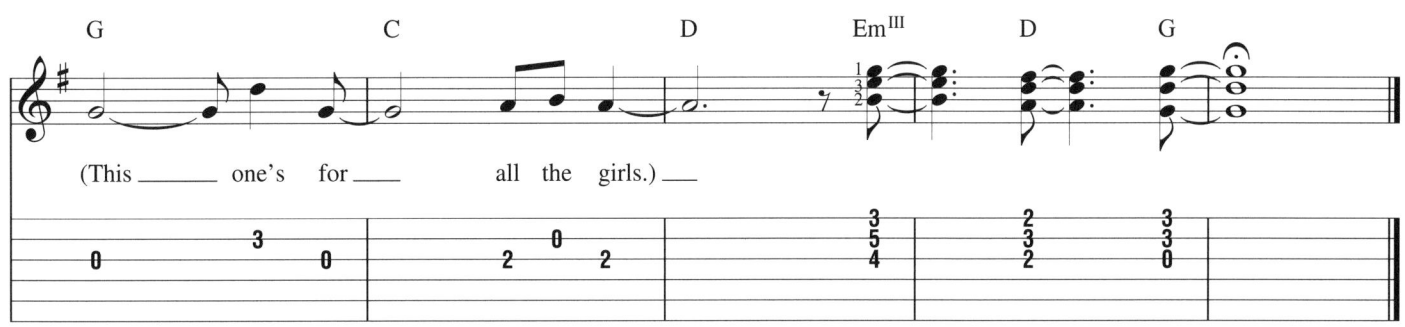

Additional Lyrics

2. This is for all you girls about twenty-five
   In little apartments, just tryin' to get by,
   Livin' on, on dreams and Spaghetti-O's,
   Wonderin' where your life's gonna go.

3. This is for all you girls about forty-two,
   Tossin' pennies in the fountain of youth.
   Every laugh, laugh line on your face
   Made you who you are today.

Travelin' Soldier

Words and Music by Bruce Robison

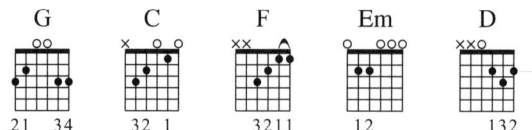

*Capo II

Strum Pattern: 3
Pick Pattern: 6

Verse
Moderately

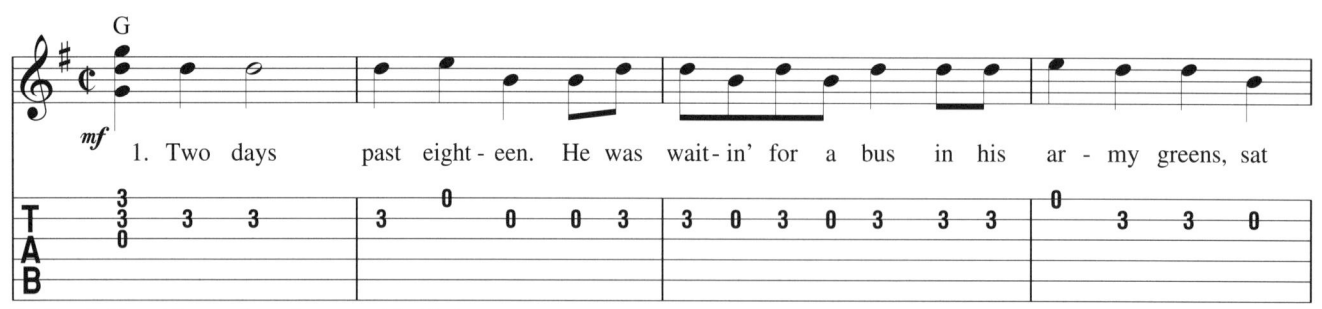

1. Two days past eighteen. He was waitin' for a bus in his army greens, sat

*Optional: To match recording, place capo at 2nd fret.

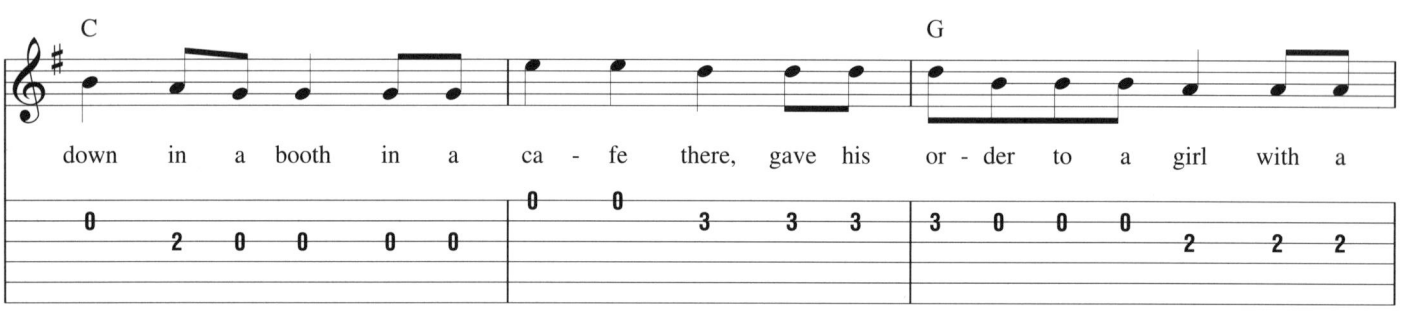

down in a booth in a cafe there, gave his order to a girl with a

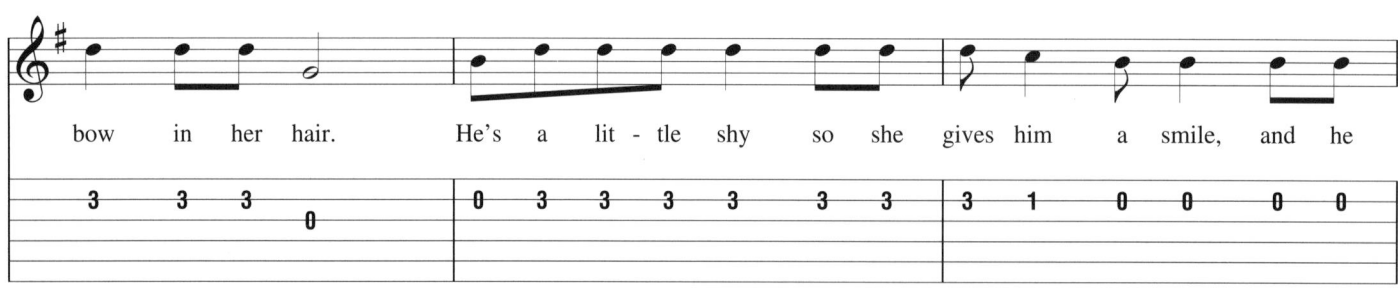

bow in her hair. He's a little shy so she gives him a smile, and he

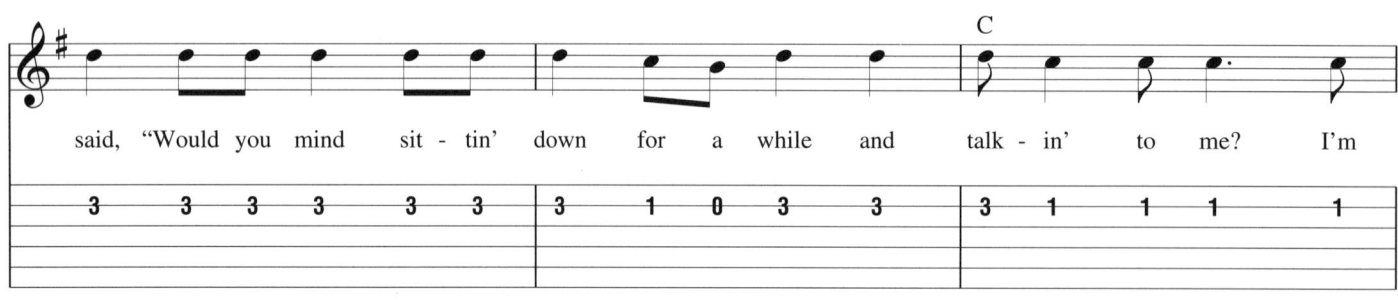

said, "Would you mind sittin' down for a while and talkin' to me? I'm

Copyright © 1999 Tiltawhirl Music (BMI) and Bruce Robison Music (BMI)
All Rights Administered by Bluewater Music Corp.
International Copyright Secured All Rights Reserved

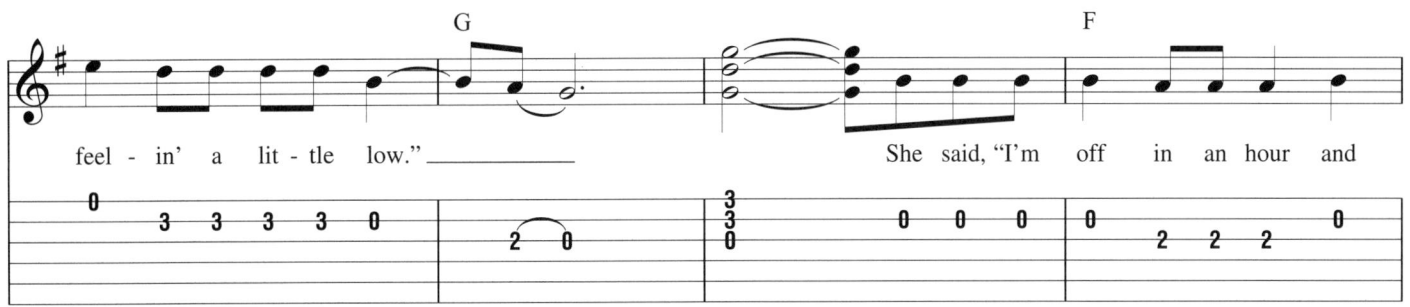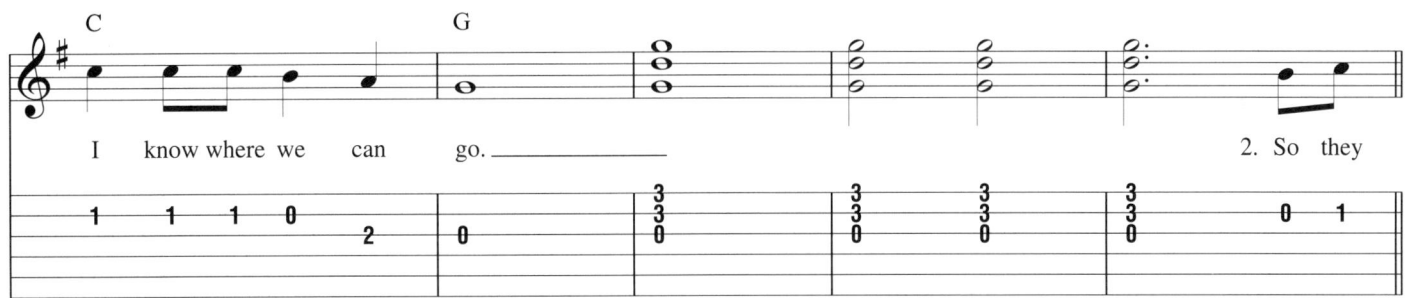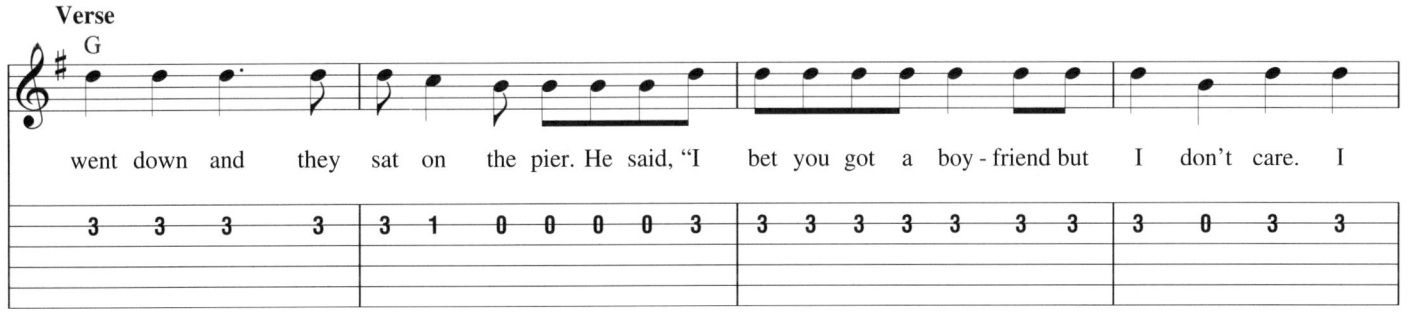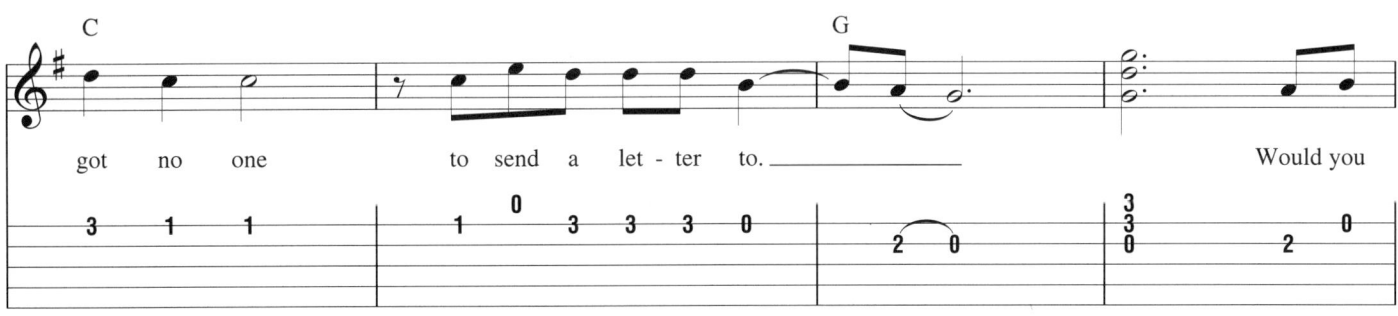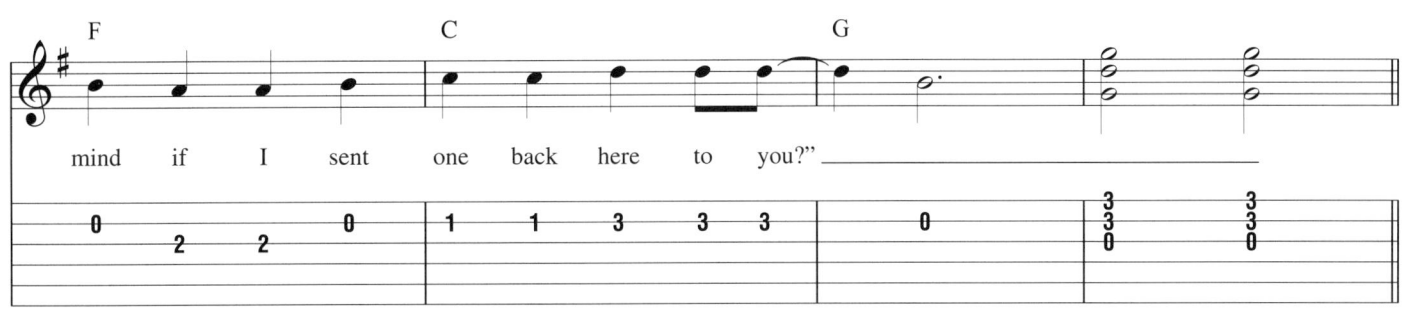

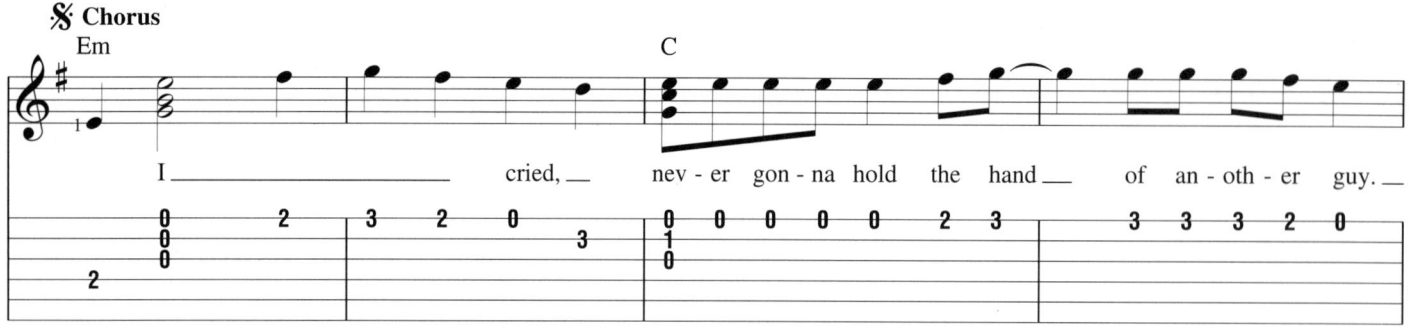
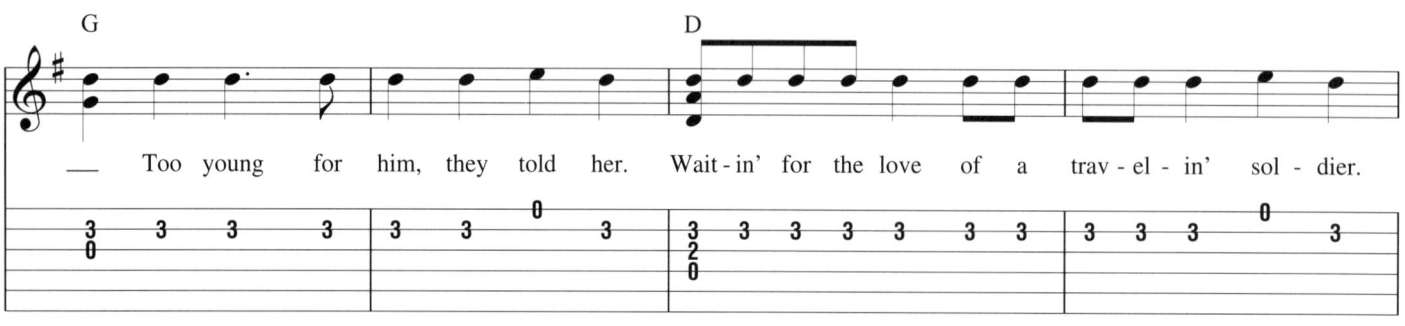
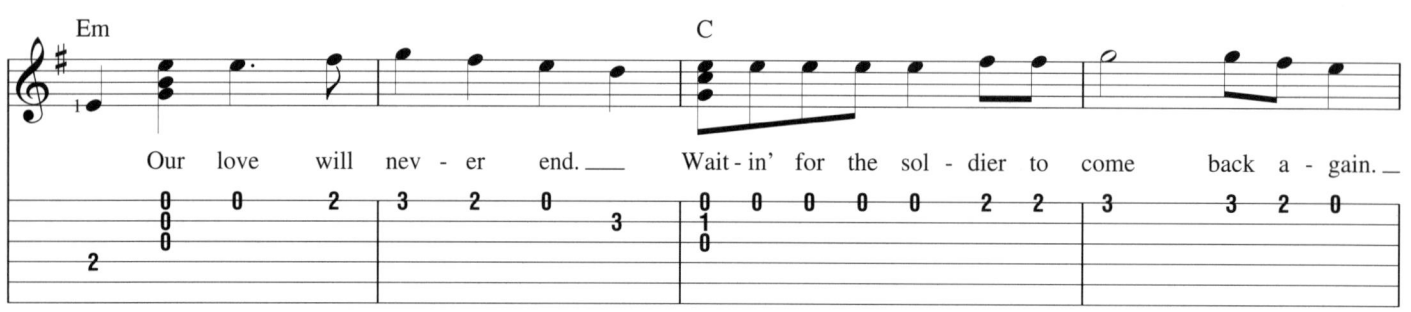
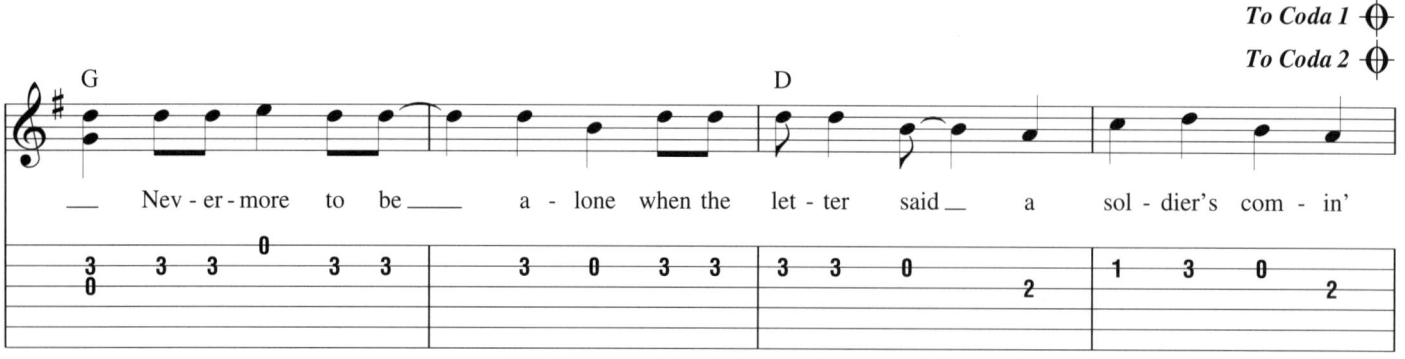

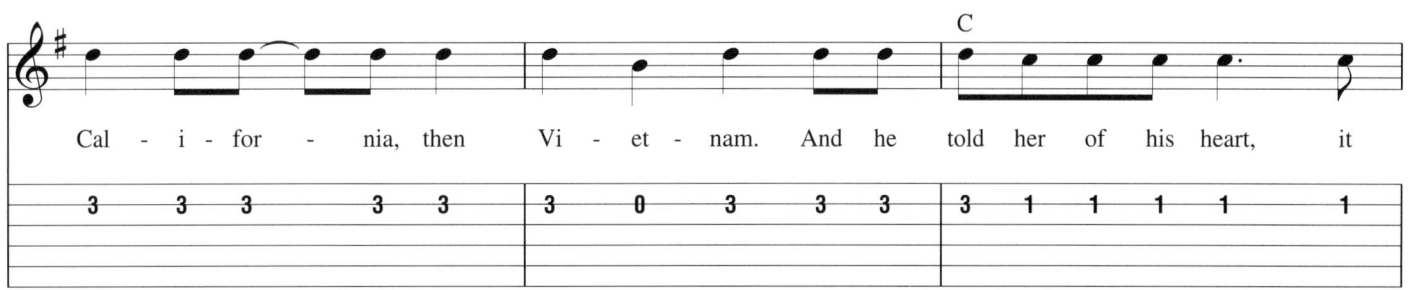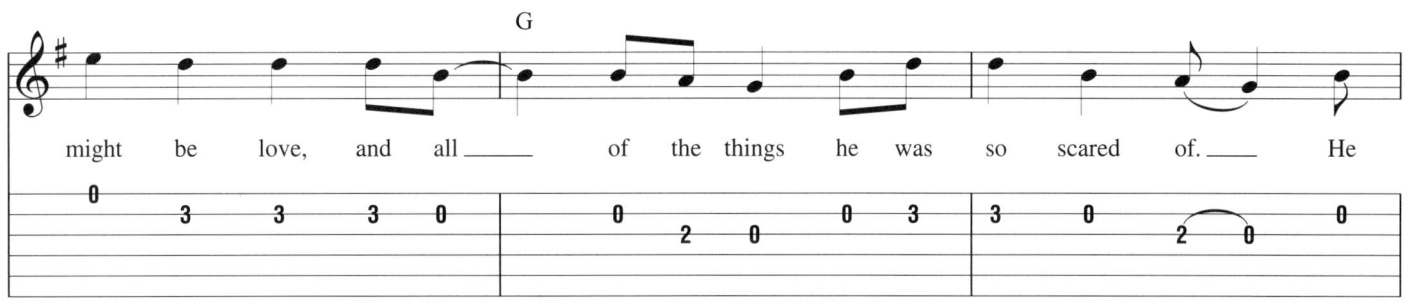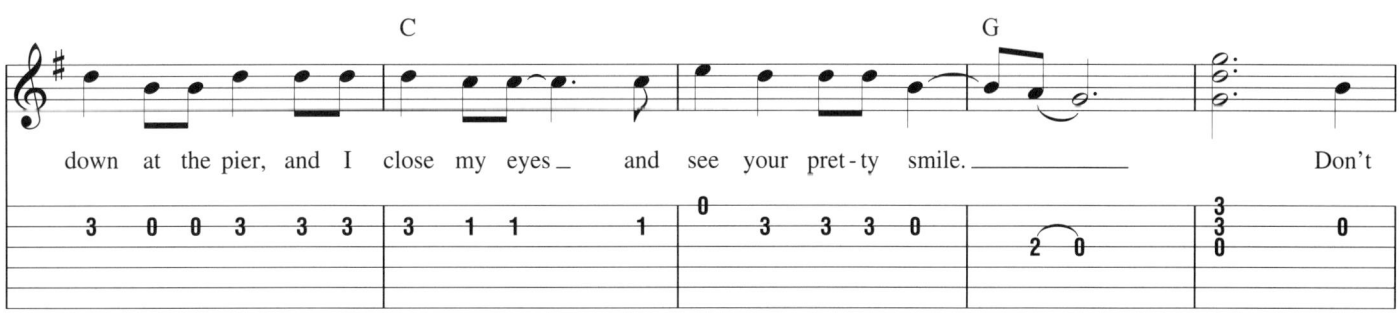

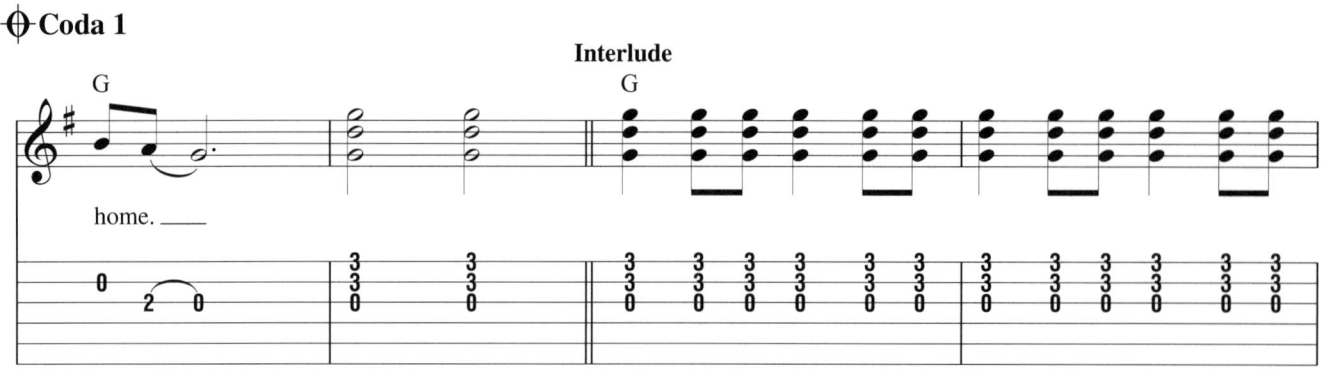
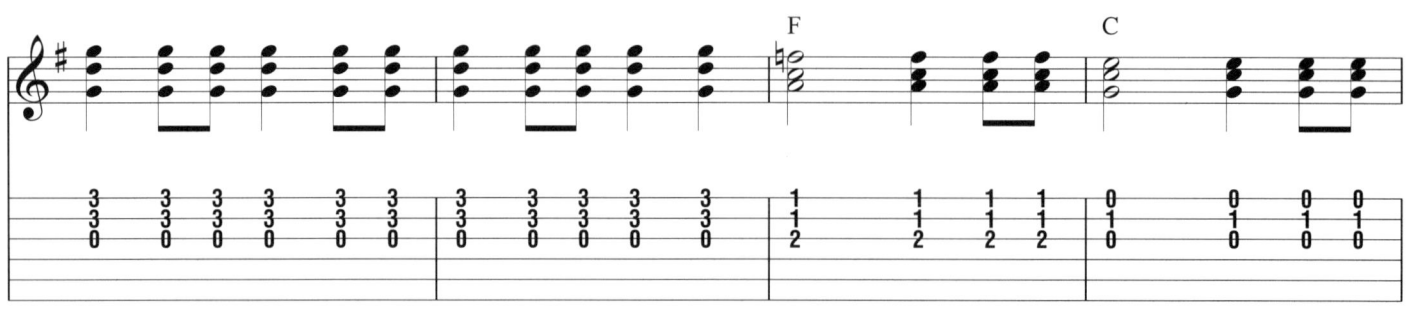
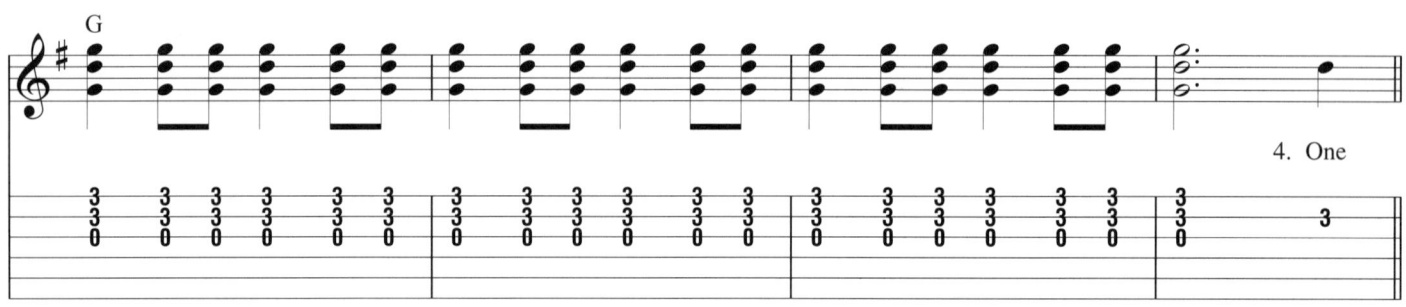
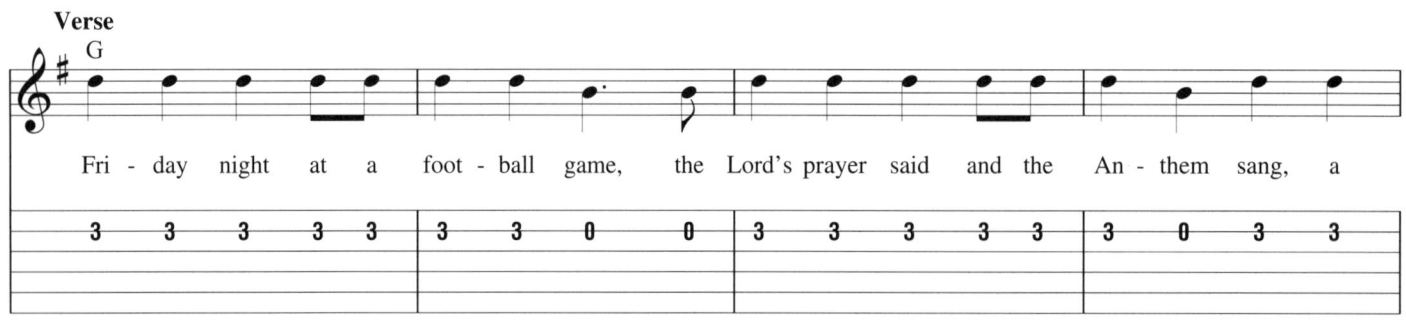
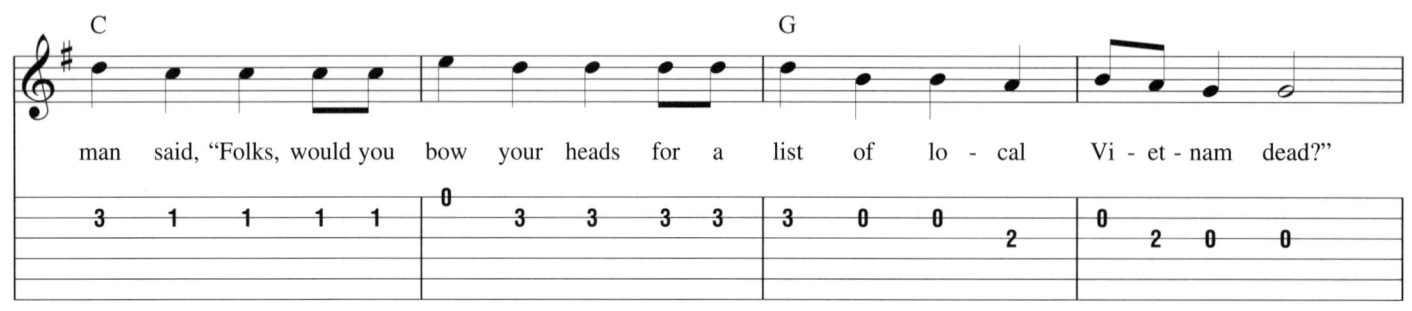

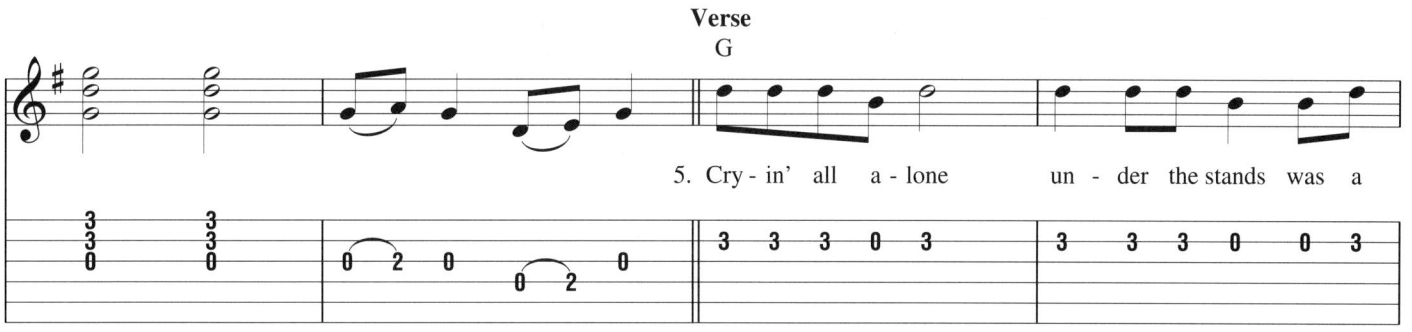
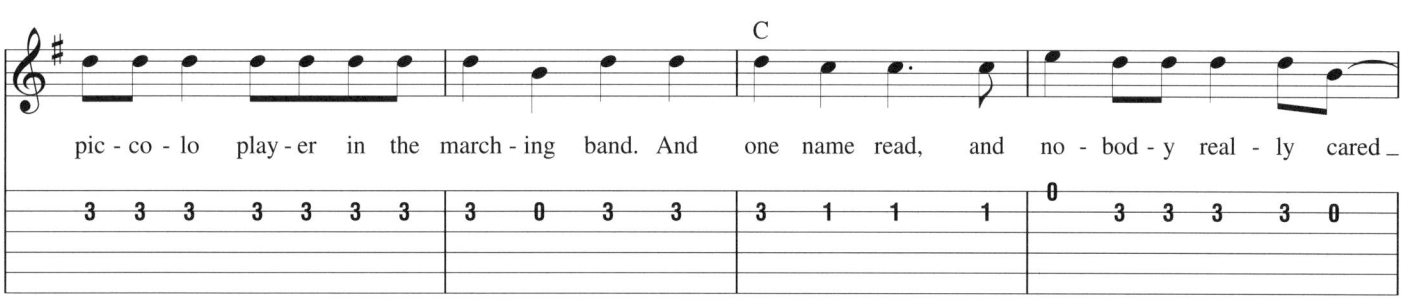
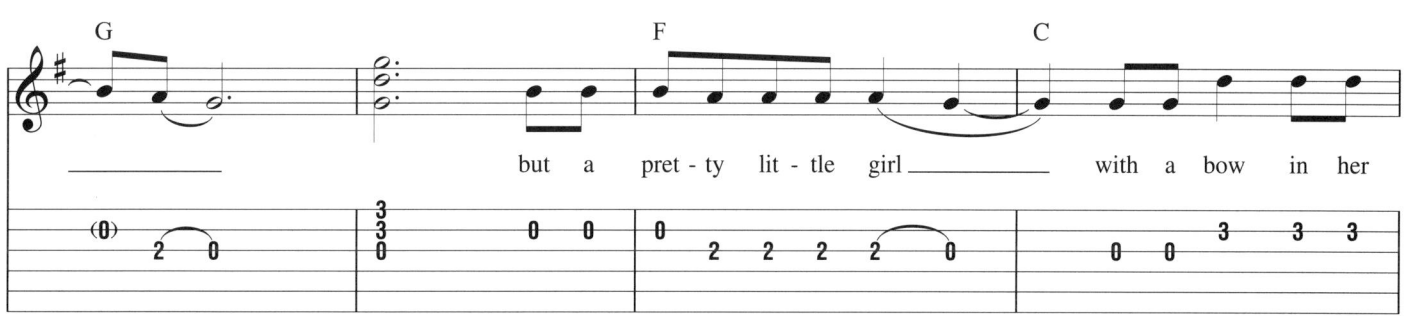
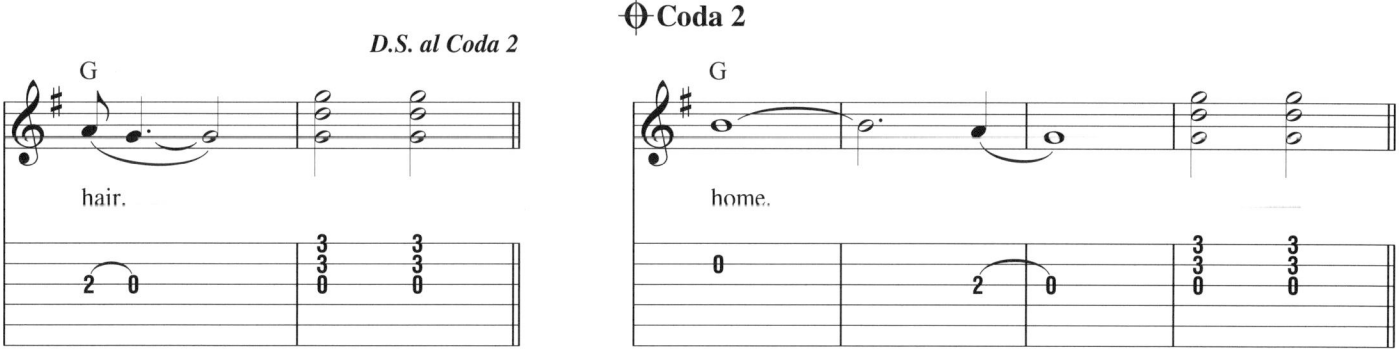
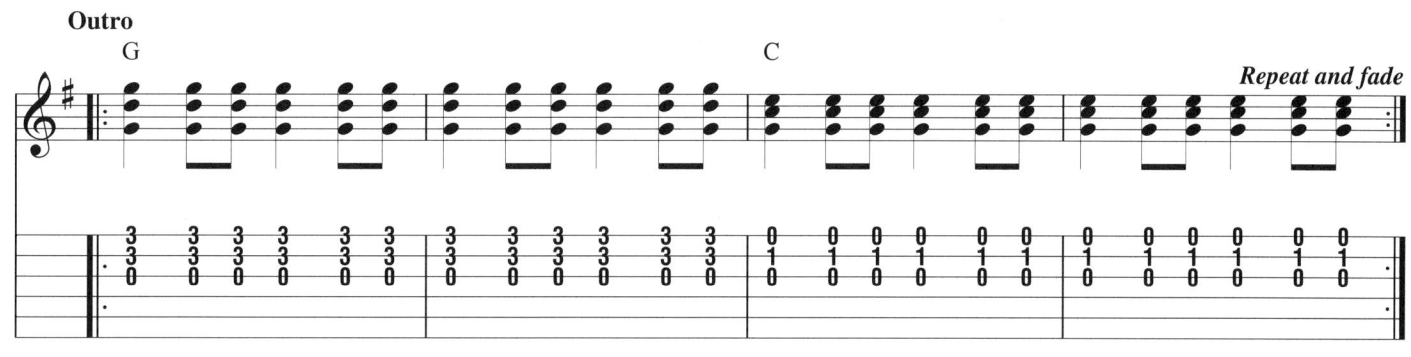

Walking in Memphis

Words and Music by Marc Cohn

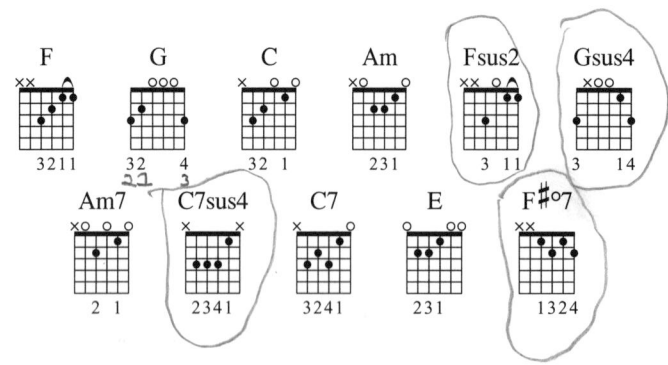

Strum Pattern: 1
Pick Pattern: 3

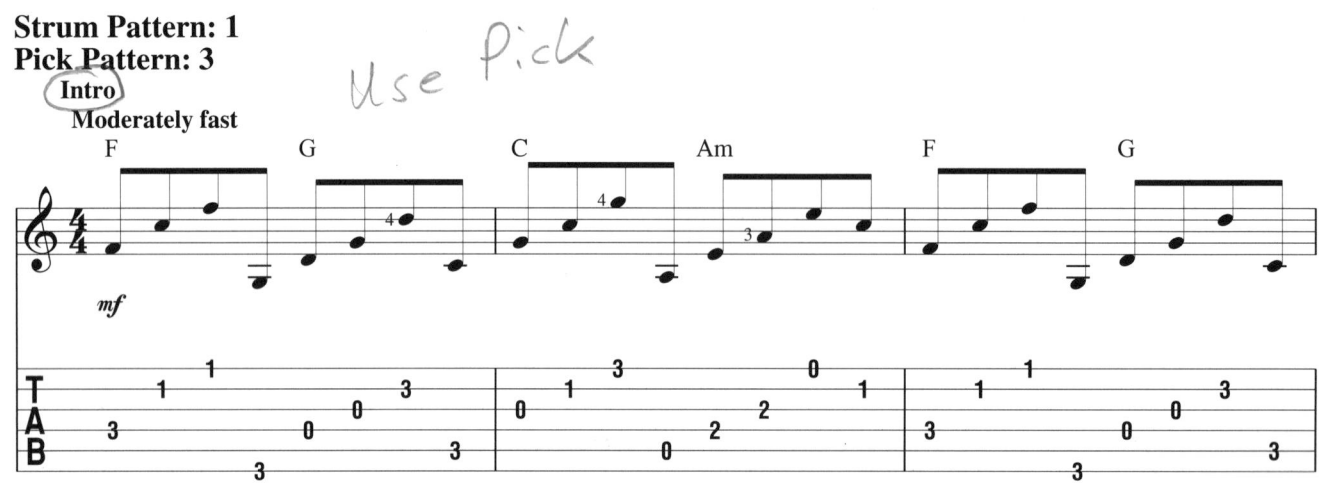

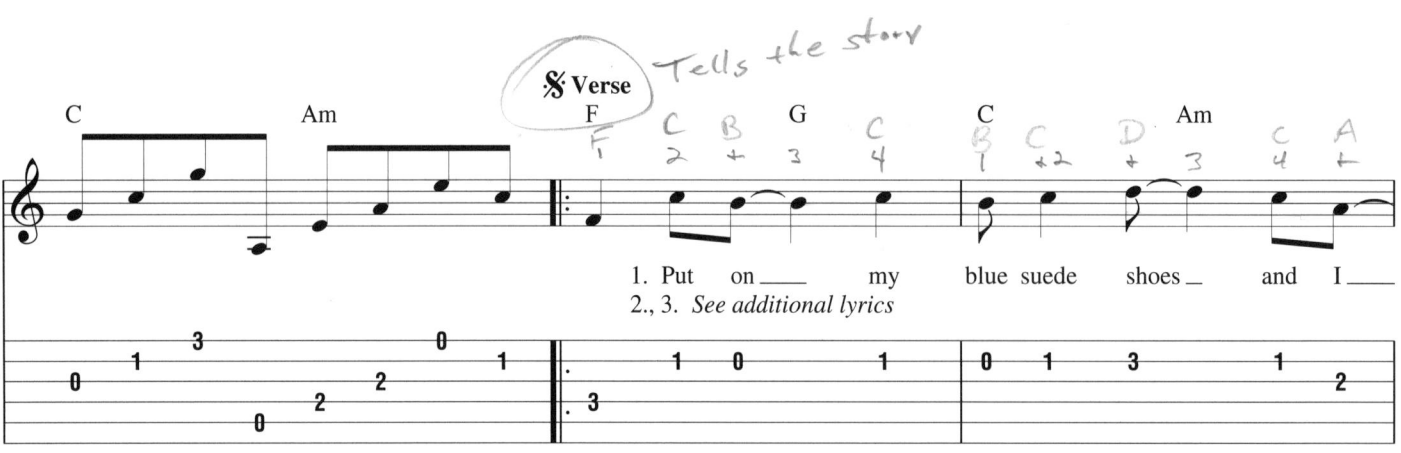

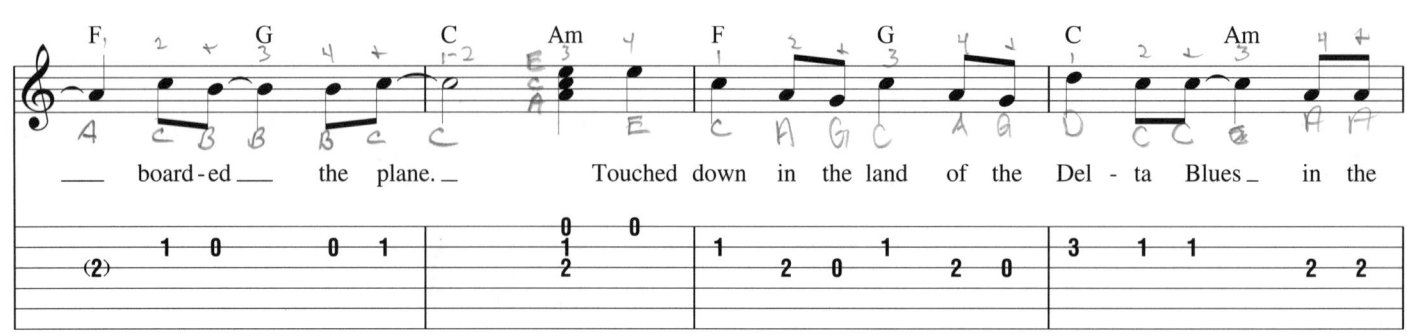

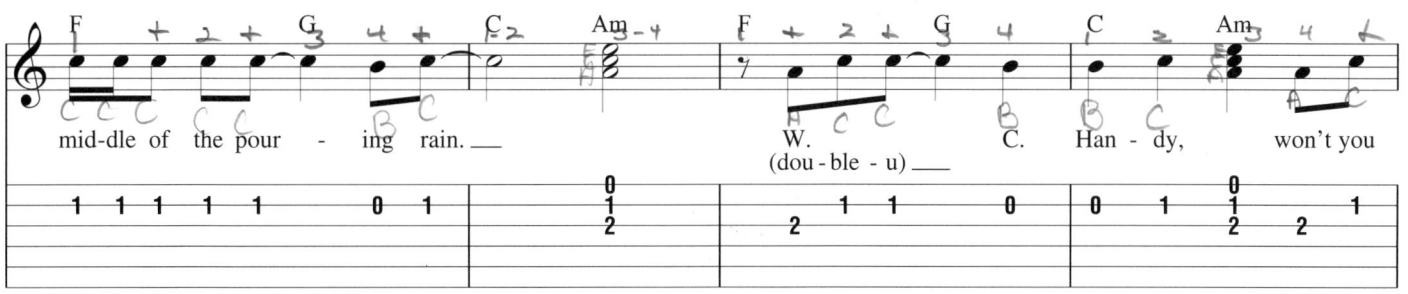

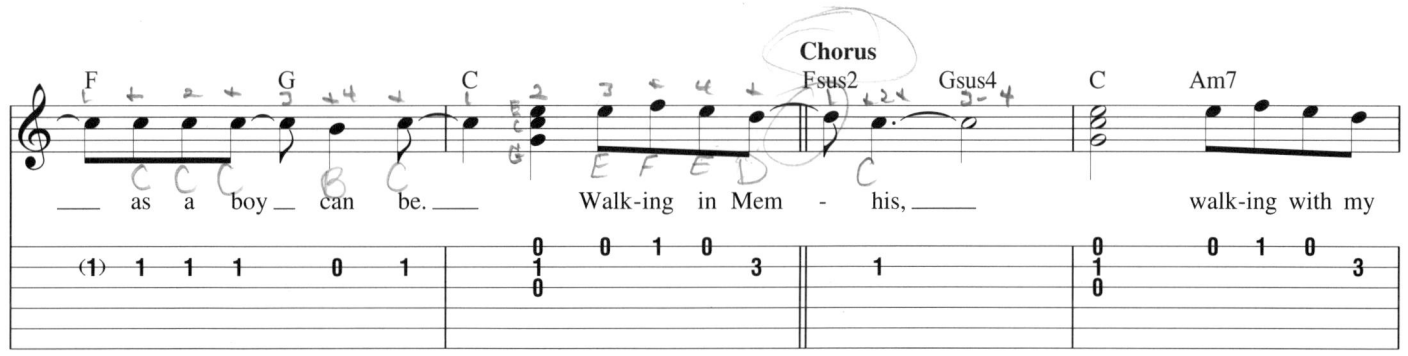
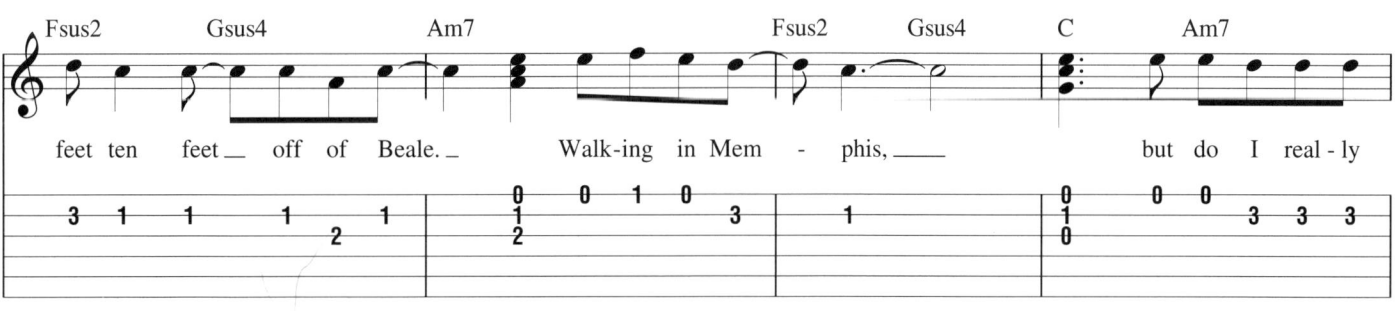
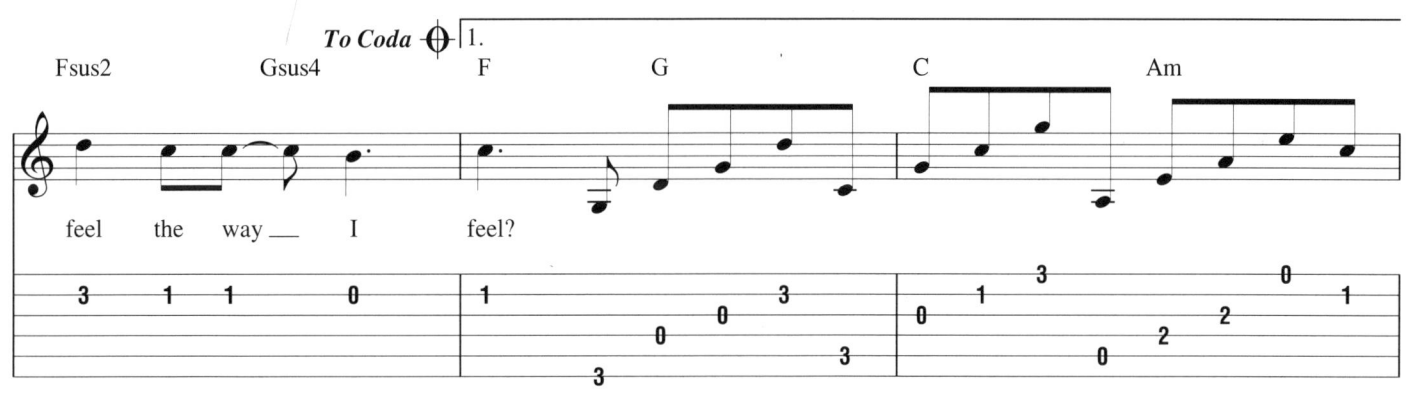

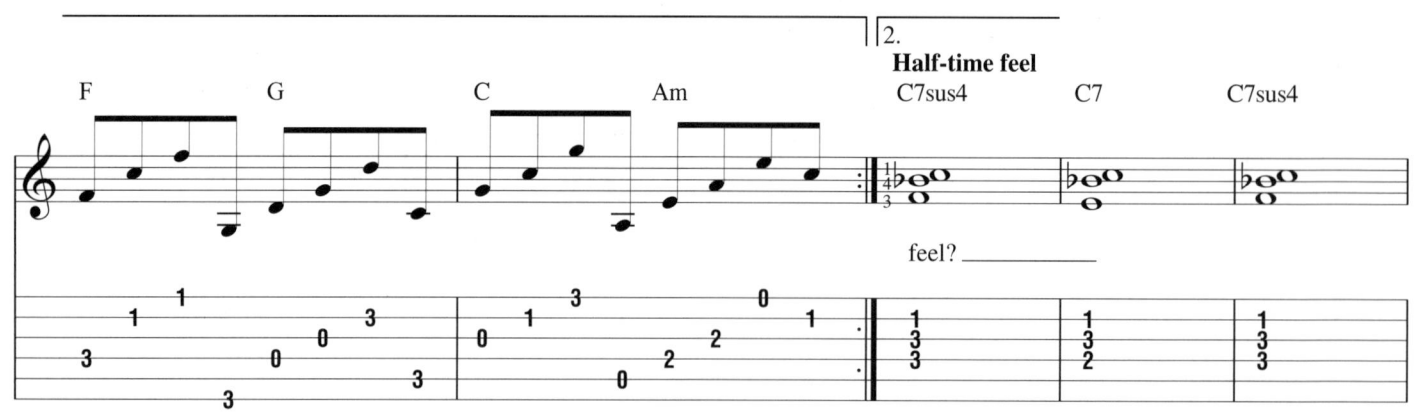

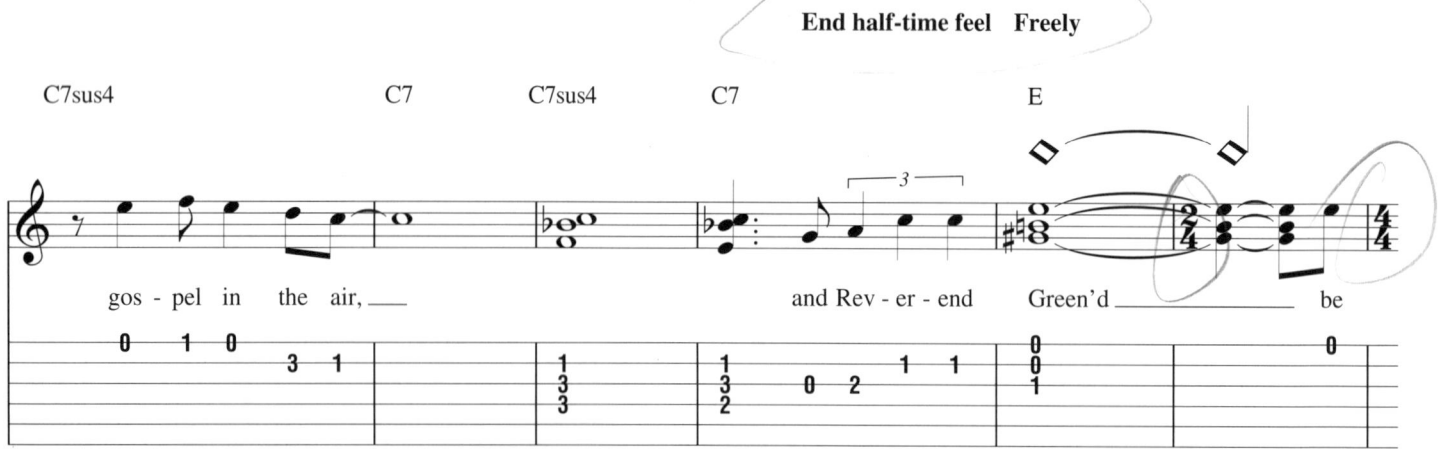

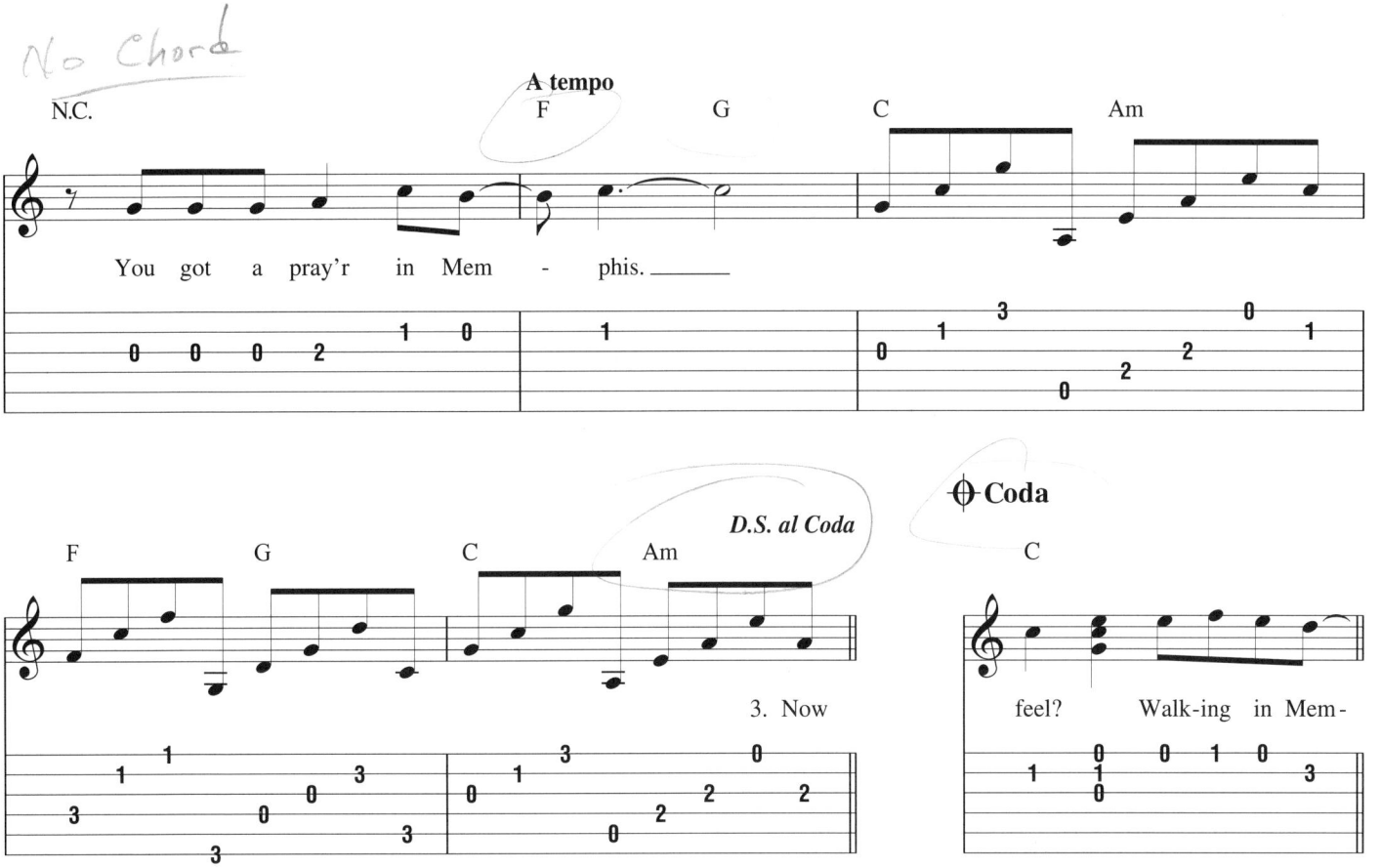
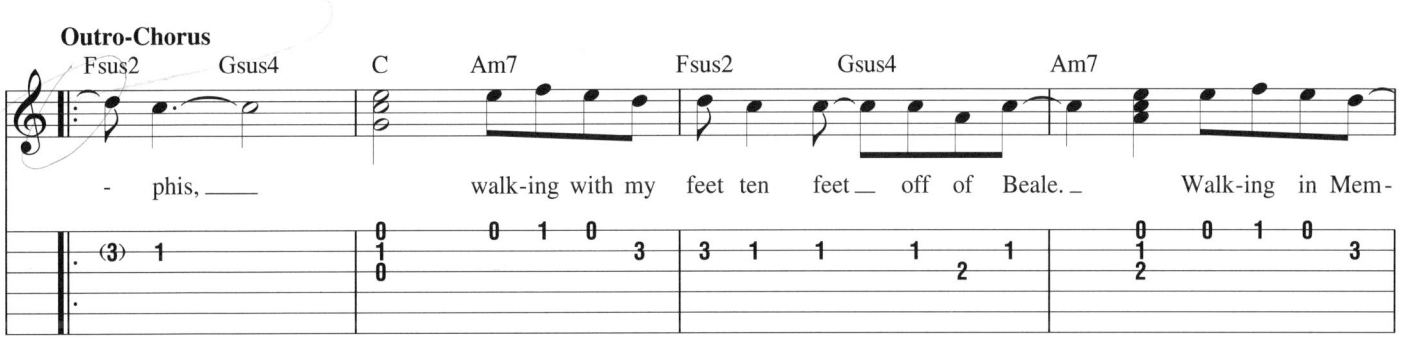

Additional Lyrics

2. Saw the ghost of Elvis down on Union Avenue.
   Followed him up to the gates of Graceland,
   And watched him walk right through.
   Now security, they did not see him;
   They just hovered 'round his tomb.
   There's a pretty little thing waiting on the King
   Down in the Jungle Room.

3. Now Muriel plays the piano ev'ry Friday at the Hollywood.
   And they brought me down to see her
   And they asked me if I would
   Do a little number,
   And I sang with all my might.
   She said, "Tell me, are you a Christian?"
   And I said, "Ma'am, I am tonight."

Party for Two

Words and Music by Shania Twain and R.J. Lange

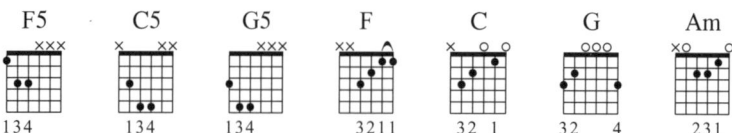

Strum Pattern: 3
Pick Pattern: 6

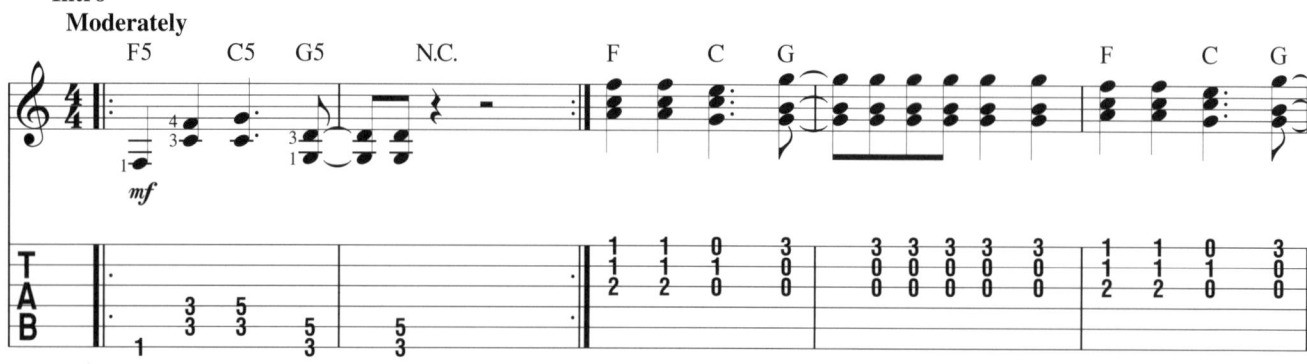

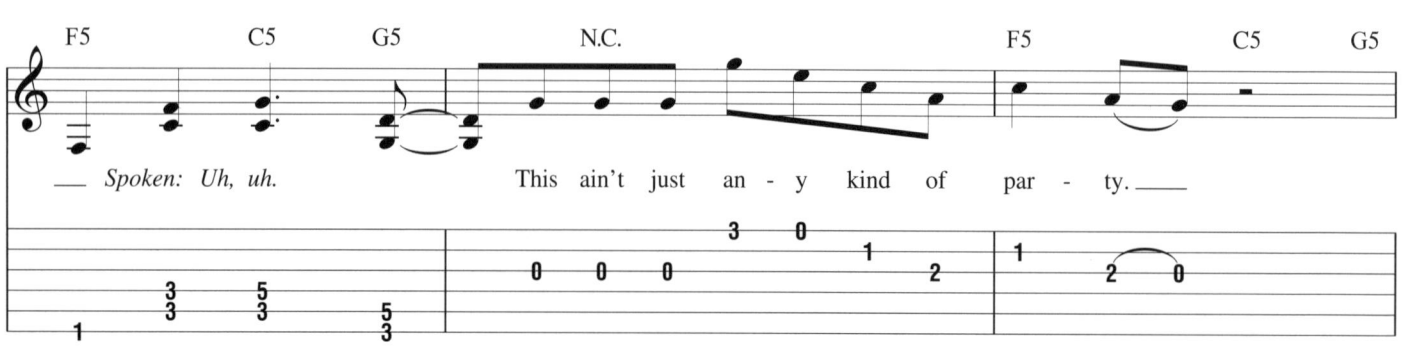

Copyright © 2004 UNIVERSAL - SONGS OF POLYGRAM INTERNATIONAL, INC., LOON ECHO, INC. and ZOMBA ENTERPRISES, INC.
All Rights for LOON ECHO, INC. Controlled and Administered by UNIVERSAL - SONGS OF POLYGRAM INTERNATIONAL, INC.
All Rights Reserved Used by Permission

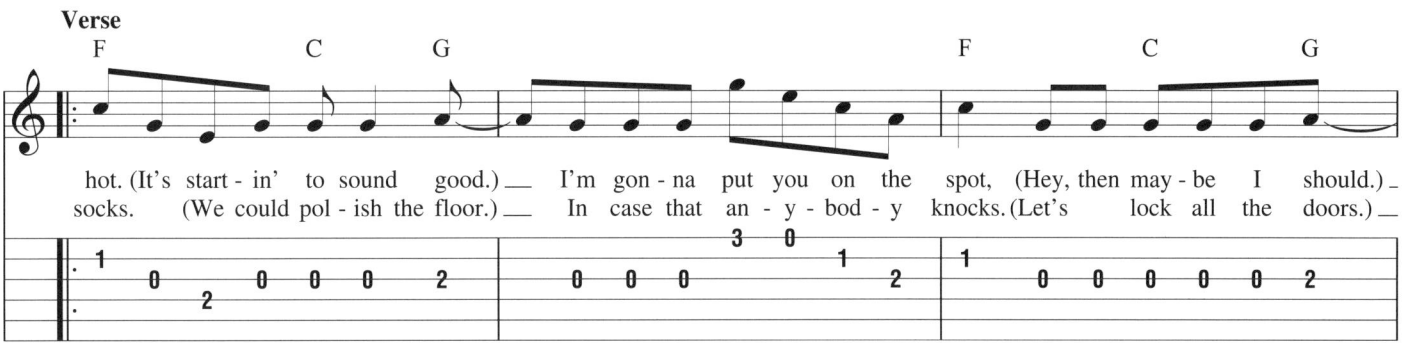
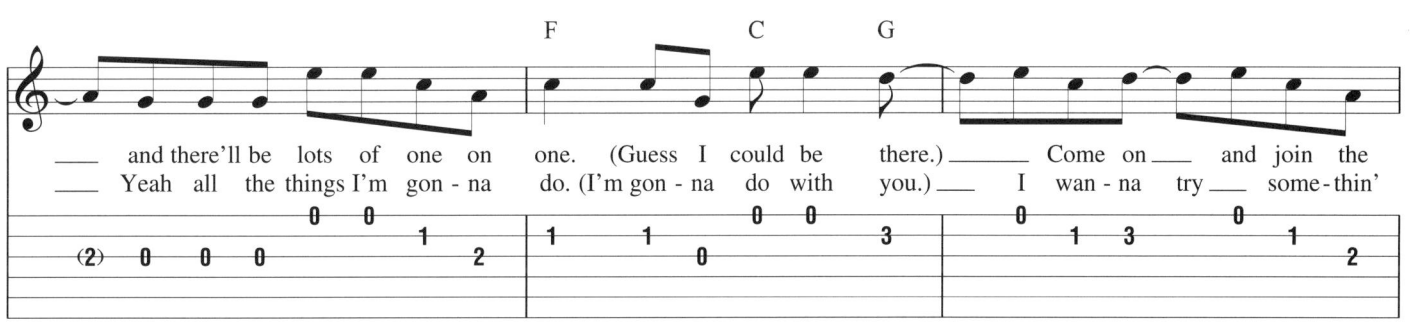

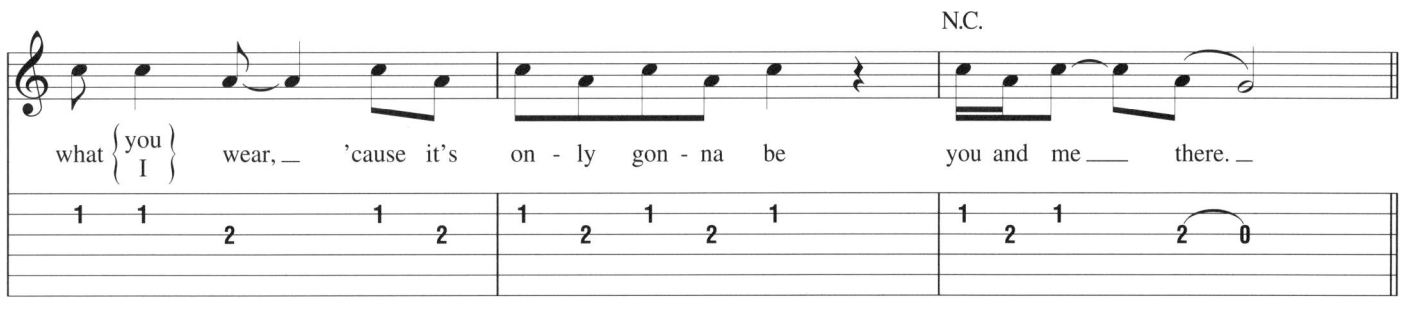

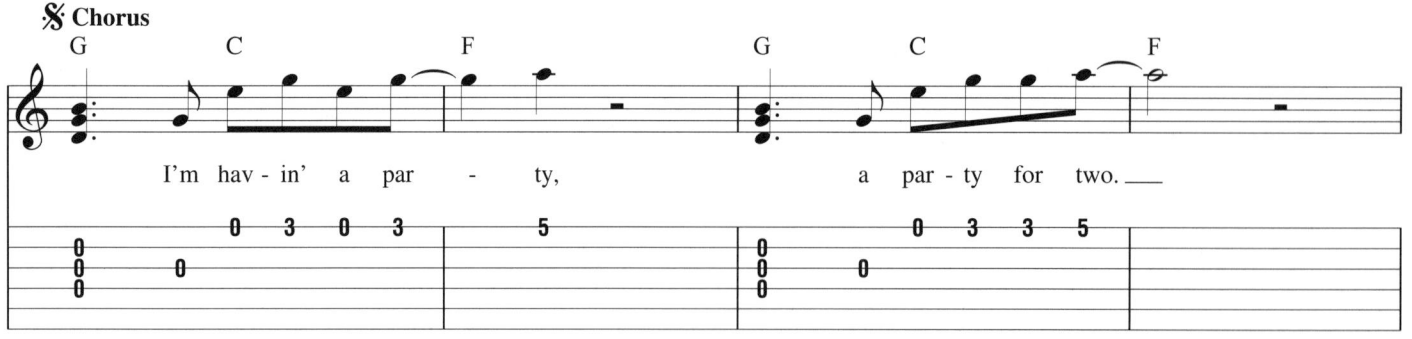
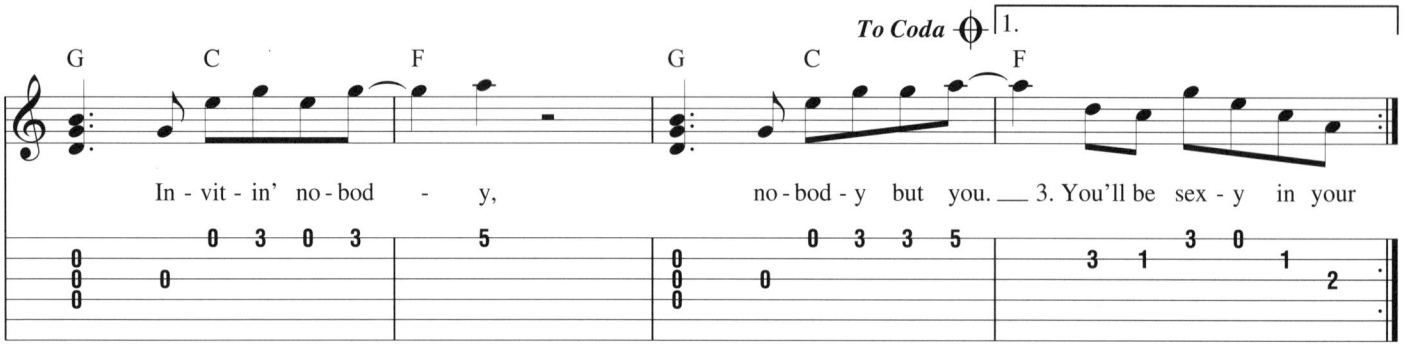

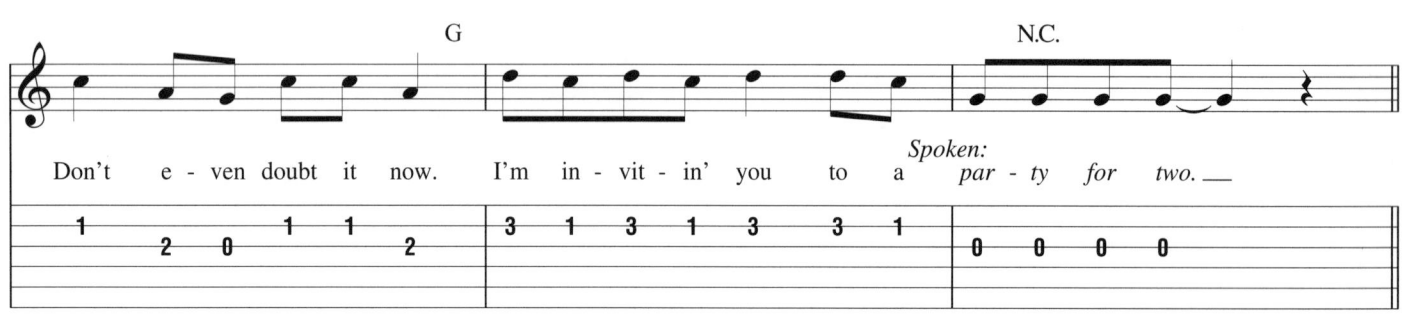

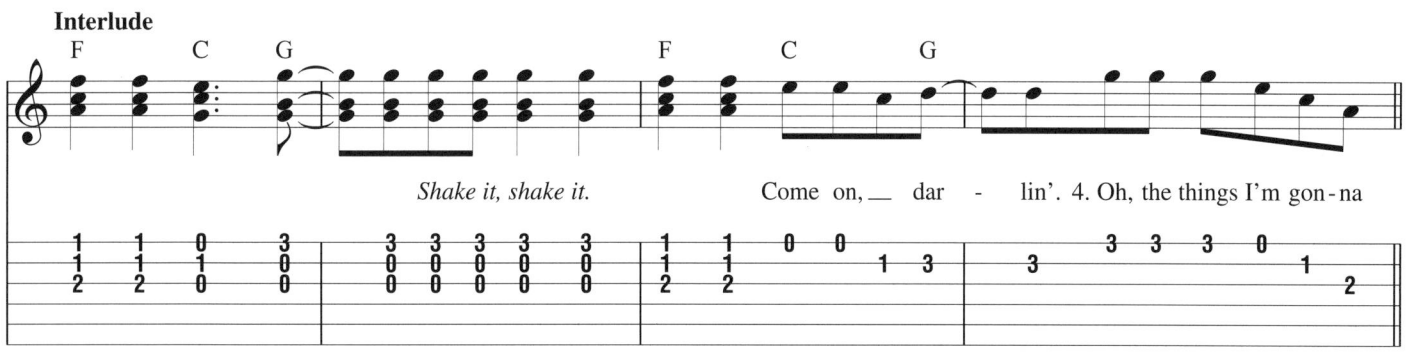
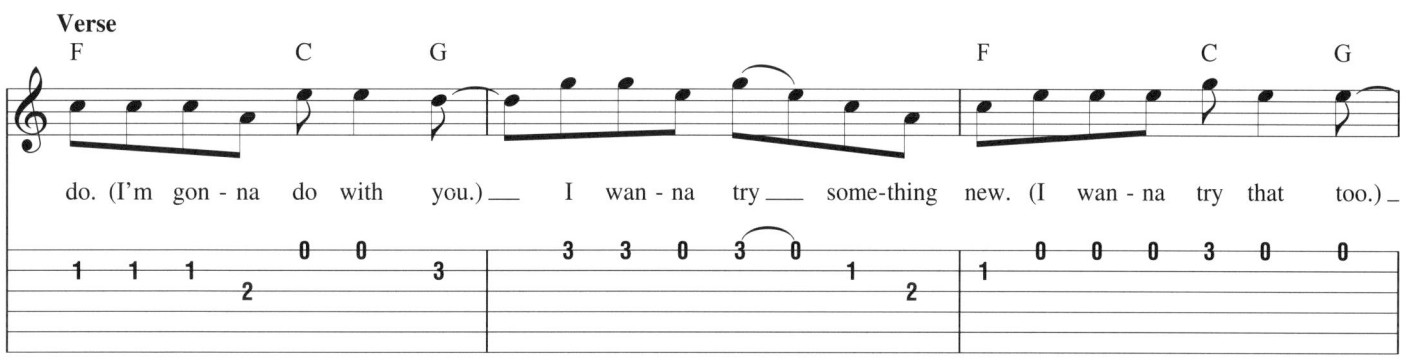
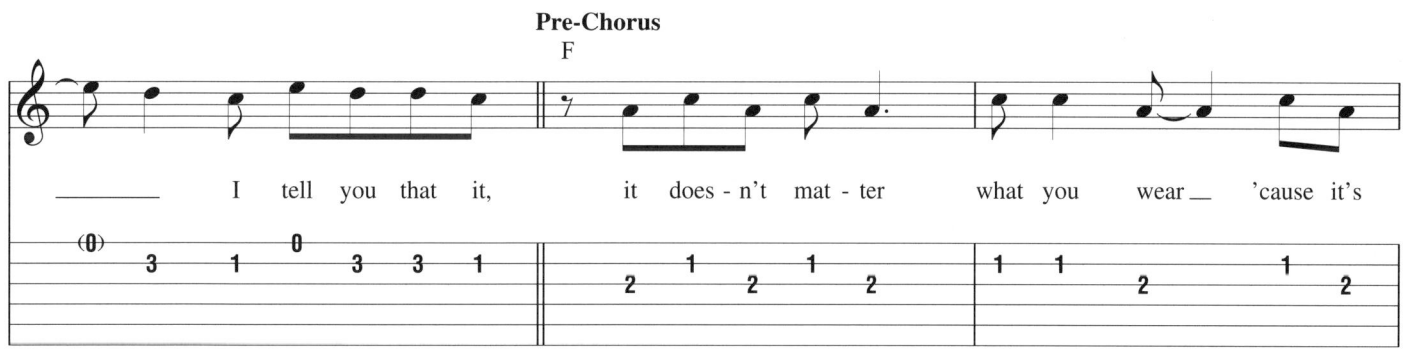
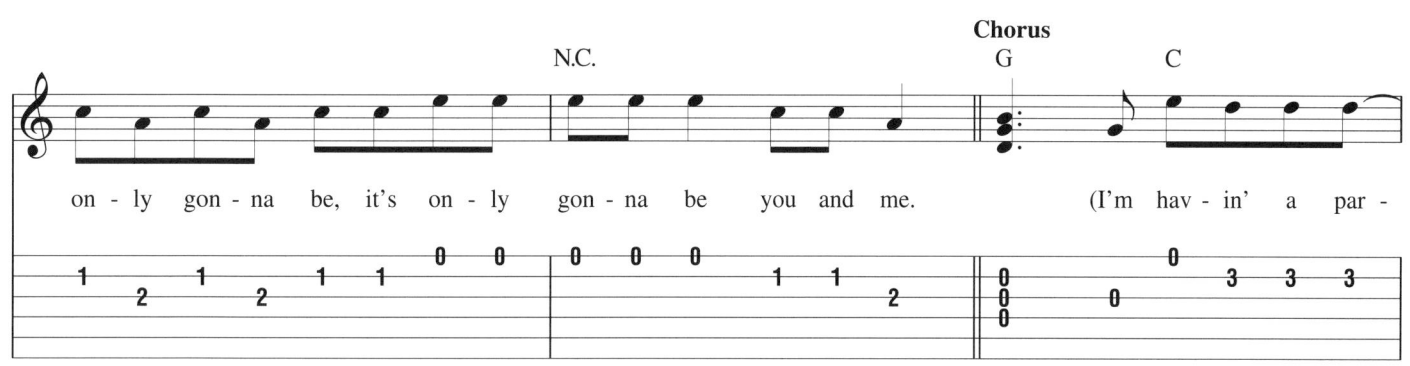

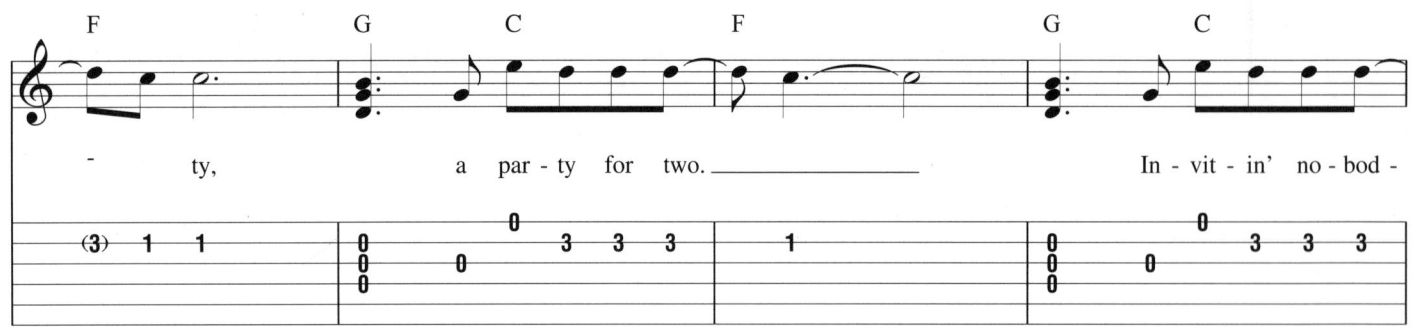
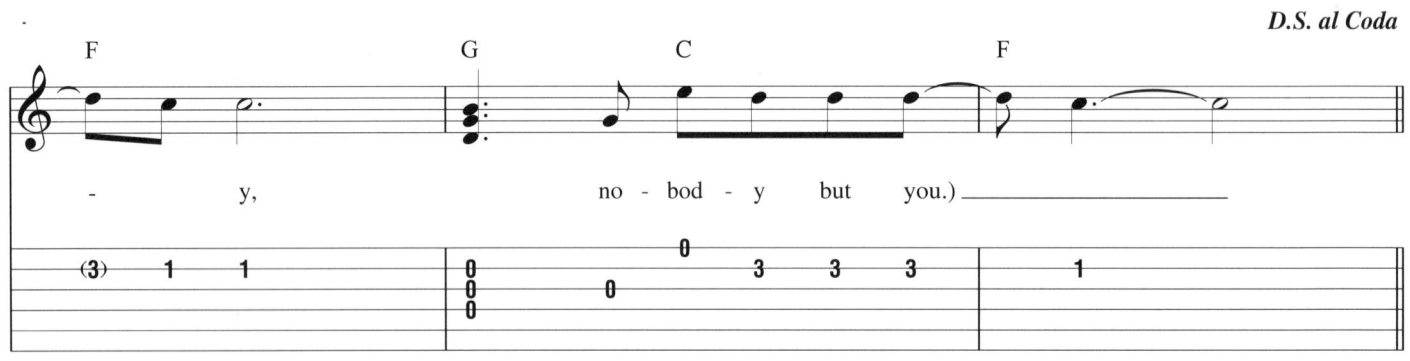
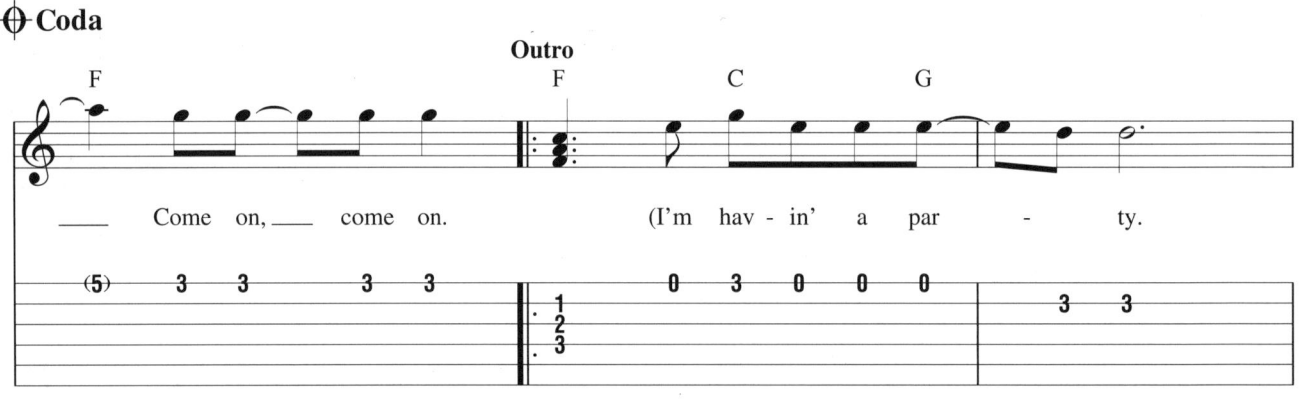
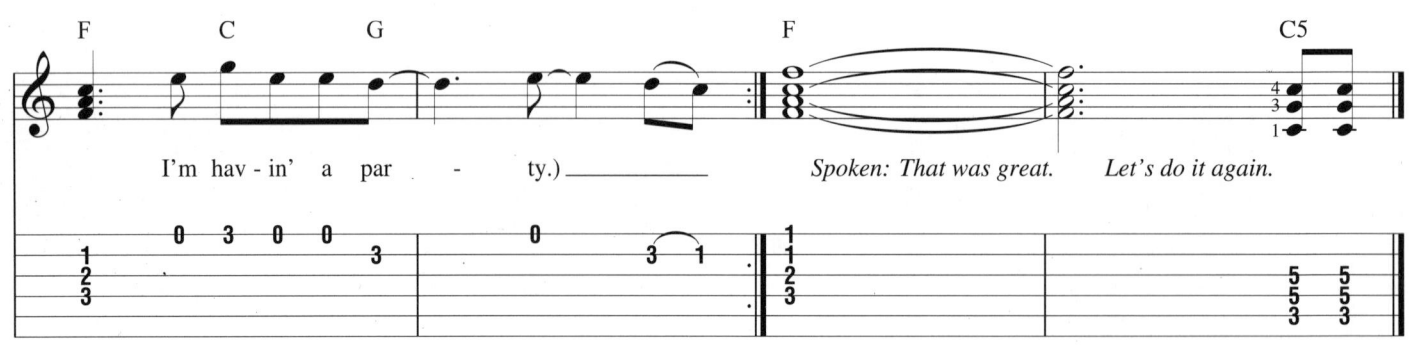